TOOLS FOR BETTER WRITING

Whether you write every day on the job or every so often at school or home, correct punctuation helps you to express your thoughts, ideas, and point of view in the clearest way possible.

This breakthrough guide strips away the confusion that often surrounds punctuation and is chock-full of easy-to-understand rules and examples that you can put into action with confidence. . . .

THE MENTOR GUIDE
TO PUNCTUATION

WILLIAM C. PAXSON is the author of three books on writing: *The Business Writing Handbook, Write It Now,* and *Principles of Style for the Business Writer.*

THE MENTOR GUIDE TO PUNCTUATION

A New, Easy-to-Use System

WILLIAM C. PAXSON

A MERIDIAN BOOK

NEW AMERICAN LIBRARY

NEW YORK AND SCARBOROUGH, ONTARIO

Copyright © 1986 by William C. Paxson

Library of Congress Catalog Card Number: 86-61330

MENTOR TRADEMARK REG. U.S. PAT. OFF. AND FOREIGN COUNTRIES
REGISTERED TRADEMARK—MARCA REGISTRADA
HECHO EN CHICAGO. U.S.A.

SIGNET, SIGNET CLASSIC, MENTOR, ONYX, PLUME, MERIDIAN AND NAL BOOKS
are published *in the United States* by New American Library,
1633 Broadway, New York, New York 10019,
in Canada by The New American Library of Canada Limited,
81 Mack Avenue, Scarborough, Ontario M1L 1M8

First Printing, October, 1986

1 2 3 4 5 6 7 8 9

PRINTED IN THE UNITED STATES OF AMERICA

Contents

A couple of hints on the importance of punctuation:

Woman without her man is a savage.

Woman, without her man, is a savage.
Woman—without her, man is a savage.
                                        —Anon.

Mr. Hall wrote that the printer's proofreader was improving my punctuation for me, & I telegraphed orders to have him shot without giving him time to pray.
    —Mark Twain, in a letter to William D. Howells

Introduction

Stop: About This Book

Stop! That's what the English call a period. To be more precise, they call a period a *full stop*. That use of terminology leaves us wondering what kind of stop there might be other than a full stop.

Anyway, I've set out to tell you about this book, so I will.

This book solves punctuation problems in the same way that you see them. Suppose you want to insert an explanatory clause into a sentence. The problem is that an explanatory clause can be marked off with commas, dashes, or parentheses. To solve this problem by using this book, check the table of contents and you'll find a listing for the problem. In this case the listing is "To Mark Off an Explanatory Element." If you turn to that section, you'll find instructions and examples that show when to use commas, dashes, or parentheses.

Accordingly, this book teaches punctuation in a manner that differs from the traditional method. The traditional method would have you checking three different chapters or sections—one on commas, one on dashes, and one on parentheses. To get the right answer by using the traditional method, you'd have to flip pages back and forth, comparing instructions and examples while mentally juggling the different rules involved.

Here, no juggling is required, for punctuation problems are solved in a logical, systematic method. I believe that you'll find the method easy to use.

Here's another example. Suppose you want to punctuate a quotation. Quotations require the use of quotation marks (double or single), introductory punctuation (commas or colons or none), ending punctuation (periods or question marks or exclamation marks), and sometimes other marks such as ellipsis points, the dots that show omission.

In this book the various problems that are part of punctuating quotations are brought together and placed in one chapter. You will not have to consult separate chapters on quotation marks, commas, colons, periods, exclamation marks, question marks, and so on.

You should also know that this book is written for anyone who writes. Here *anyone* means the professional writer or editor, the person who writes on the job regardless of job title, and the student in high school or college.

That usefulness exists for several reasons. One, examples come from a variety of sources in business and technical writing and from the works of the best of contemporary authors. Two, instructions are presented in language that is generally free of special grammatical terms; if special terminology is used, it is defined where it is introduced or in the mini-glossary at the end of the introduction. Three, instructions are based upon the punctuation practices followed in the popular press and in a variety of professions; the bibliography at the end of the book is a guide to the sources of these practices.

In addition, the book shows you how to handle related matters such as capitalization and spacing.

And I have tried not to be arbitrary and dogmatic in presenting rules and principles governing punctuation. That is, where optional styles exist, I have presented the options.

The result is a book that can be used when writing fiction, nonfiction, scholarly papers, scientific treatises, themes or essays for school work, business letters, or letters to friends and relatives.

One more point: The book teaches American practice, not English. The differences are minor. As an example, American practice uses double quotation marks first, then single; English practice is the opposite. Don't ask why. These two systems are different, and that's all there is to it.

Start: How to Use This Book

To get the most benefit out of this book, remember that your starting point is punctuation purpose and not a specific punctuation mark. Then follow these steps:

1. Decide what purpose you want to use punctuation for. Do you want to introduce a quotation? Add emphasis to a word? Punctuate an interjection? Use punctuation to separate thoughts?
2. Then consult the listing of punctuation purposes in the table of contents. If you can't find what you're looking for there, check the index.
3. Turn to the page given. Read the instructions, and see how punctuation is used in the examples.
4. If the text shows optional styles of punctuation, pick one style and stick with it. Be consistent. Consistency saves you time, and readers have faith in writers who are consistent in their attention to detail.

The steps just given are the minimum steps necessary for the quick and efficient use of this book. I also recommend that you read the remainder of the introduction, for it covers the development of punctuation, some special uses of punctuation, the importance of the subject, and a few special terms used in the book.

When using this book, keep in mind the differences between typewritten and typeset material. Concerning punctuation, these differences have to do with the dash and italic type.

A dash is made on a typewriter by striking the hyphen key twice. On some word processing equipment a special key is available for typing the dash. When this key is available, it should be used.

As for *italic type*, it is indicated by underlining in a typewritten manuscript. If the manuscript is printed, the typesetter converts underlined passages to italics.

A Brief History Lesson: Punctuation, the Oral Tradition, and Writing

We can trace our system of punctuation back to the systems used in ancient Greece and Rome. In those civilizations, few people read, with one exception being the orator. Standing before hundreds or thousands of listeners, the orator, when not speaking from memory, read from a prepared speech. Because no one can ramble on forever without breathing, orators quickly developed a system of marks on the page that showed them when to do just that—stop to take a breath. In time the system was expanded to show when to pause for minor effect, when to pause for greater effect, and when to raise the voice and ask a question.

Accordingly, what developed at the outset was a system of punctuation used strictly for oral purposes. The speech had to sound right. Punctuation was addressed to the ear, not the eye.

A space was the easiest punctuation to put, or leave, on the page. Spacing was supplemented with dots on the page—"points." From the Latin *punctus*, "point," comes the word *punctuation*. And because punctuation was planned to cause the reader to stop, the word *stop* also came into play.

Chaucer may have been the first writer in English to call attention to punctuation when in 1386 he wrote, "And here a point, for ended is my tale." Although that particular tale may have ended, interest in punctuation continued, and by the 17th century the words *stop* and *punctuation* were widely used by writers, printers, and virtually anyone who felt like commenting on the English language.

As printing and literacy increased, punctuation for oral effect proved that it left a lot to be desired. Sentences ran on and on, seemingly forever, when they appeared in print. Readers grew weary of waiting for the period and had a hard time deciphering what was meant.

Moreover, no standard of punctuation existed, a situation that led to interminable quarrels among printers and writers.

In time, punctuation for oral effect gave way to a different system, and the two systems can be described as *elocutionary* and *grammatical*. The older system was elocutionary, concentrated on the spoken word, and tended to be rhythmical; the older system pertained to how the writing sounded. The newer system is grammatical and syntactical and tends to be logical; the newer system, the one predominating today, pertains to what the writing means.

In addition, modern punctuation tends to be more uniform, while older punctuation had no such tendency at all.

As the systems changed over the centuries, so did the marks. The period was once an elevated dot (·), but moved down to take its place on the line. The question mark came into being to replace the Greek mark that looks like our semicolon, and we assigned other uses to the semicolon. The virgule (/) split. One part remained as a virgule, and the other part slid down to the line, took on a curve, and became the comma.

Out of this apparent confusion came a system of marks that today is fairly well standardized.

Still, it is a system in which writers have room to maneuver. Some writers use little punctuation, some use much, and both categories seem able to get their points across. Newspaper style of punctuation is considerably different from the style seen in scientific journals. Writers of fiction can be casual with punctuation, if they want to be, while writers of nonfiction often find that their topics demand precise punctuation.

Punctuation in this country is not the same as it is in the British Isles. What we call "marks" British publications speak of as "points" and "stops." Our use of quotation marks is not the same as British use, and our use of punctuation in general adheres to guidelines that are more rigid than those followed by British publishers and writers—and yet we can still understand each other.

Variety abounds. Poets sometimes use punctuation to impart rhythm to passages, as if providing a beat to music. Tom Wolfe wrote of his style that "things like exclamation points, italics, and abrupt shifts (dashes) and syncopations (dots) helped to give the illusion not only of a person talking but of a person thinking" (*The New Journalism*, Harper & Row, 1973).

The various uses of punctuation extend into the sciences. With some computer programs, three periods at the end of one sentence are signals that another sentence is coming, and a virgule prefixes a command. In chemistry, hyphens show a known sequence in an amino acid chain, for example, *Ala-Leu-Lys*; to the chemist, each hyphen indicates a peptide bond, something that is meaningless to the rest of us. Unknown sequences are enclosed in parentheses with the symbols separated by commas, as in (*Gly, Phe, Tyr*).

Regardless of the present variety and regardless of the probability that still other uses of punctuation might someday appear, it is well to keep in mind that punctuation developed as a means of helping readers understand what they were reading and that such help should still be its purpose.

Motivation Step: Is the Subject Important?

Teachers are taught the importance of a *motivation step*. The purpose of a motivation step is to impress upon students the importance of the subject, the value of studying it, and what is to be gained by learning it.

So, as far as punctuation is concerned, is the subject important?

As an answer to that question, consider the following episode. It concerns a debate that took place in the U.S. Congress early in 1977 and was reported in the *Congressional Record* of March 4 of the same year.

S. I. Hayakawa started the debate in question. Hayakawa possessed varied talents: semanticist, best-selling author, college professor and administrator, and U.S. senator from California. On a Friday afternoon in March of 1977, Hayakawa rose on the Senate floor to present what he called a "close microanalysis" of a "tedious grammatical point." The tedious grammatical point concerned the use of commas with nonessential clauses.

A particular comma was being discussed, one attributed to Paul C. Warnke, President Carter's nominee to be chief U.S. delegate to the Strategic Arms Limitation Talks (SALT) with the Soviet Union. Warnke was accused of deleting a comma from a rather important sentence. The original version of the sentence, written in 1972, read:

> There is no purpose in either side's achieving a numeri-
> cal superiority, which is not translatable into either any
> sort of military capability or any sort of political potential.

With the comma, the clause beginning "which is" is nones-sential; that is, the clause can be removed from the sentence without altering the basic meaning of the sentence. If the clause can be removed, then the basic meaning of Warnke's sentence is that numerical weapons superiority serves no purpose.

But in 1977 Warnke said that he wrote a different sentence, and in 1977 he even added the emphasis shown:

> I specifically stated [in 1972] that "nuclear superiority
> *which is not translatable into any sort of military capa-
> bility or any sort of political potential* has no purpose."

Without commas around it, the italicized clause beginning "which is" is essential to the meaning of the sentence. Warnke's 1977 version argued that numerical superiority could be important.

In short, the two versions presented considerably different meanings.

The two meanings were thrashed around in a debate that had its humorous moments. Hayakawa and several other senators discussed the punctuation of essential and nonessen-tial clauses, with Hayakawa getting a laugh when he said, "I have not had so much fun teaching grammar in 20 years." And Senator Russell Long demonstrated an excellent grasp of the obvious when he remarked, "Most of us, when we make a speech, do not say the comma."

Humor aside, Warnke's credibility was severely damaged. The debate leading to his confirmation occupied four days and was often acrimonious. And it was not a lot of fuss over just any old comma. In this case the comma said a lot about the thought processes of one particular man, a man about to be appointed to a very critical position.

Punctuation is associated with other disasters or near disasters. Among them is the case of King Edward II, who is said to have been executed because of an errant comma. Then there is the story of the Irishman Roger Casement. Casement was brought to trial on charges of treason during World War I. He was convicted in short order, and his lawyers appealed the sentence on the interpretation of a virgule. The court applied its interpretation to the virgule, and Casement lost and was hanged.

In this country, a group of civil service examinees punctuated a test sentence with a question mark, a style of punctuation that caused them to fail the examination. They appealed to the New York Supreme Court, won, and were given passing grades.

Some punctuation abuses merely make the reader work harder. A case in point is the opening sentence of George Orwell's essay "Marrakech." Orwell, always the striver for clarity, somehow wasn't watching his commas when he wrote, "As the corpse went past the flies left the restaurant table in a cloud and rushed after it." Put a comma after "past," and the sentence need not be read twice to figure out what is going on.

Other punctuation problems are minor errors, more in the nature of temporary distractions or slight embarrassments. One in this category concerns the affliction named for the English doctor Langdon Down, who in 1866 described the physical features of children who were first called *mongoloids*. Later the affliction became known as *Down's syndrome*, with the possessive apostrophe. In more recent years, health professionals have dropped the apostrophe, their reason being that Dr. Down never had the disorder himself and therefore the possessive is inaccurate. Today the correct term is *Down syndrome* (*Discover*, February 1985).

These little object lessons are important. You use punctuation to serve readers, to guide them to the correct understanding of your thoughts. You use punctuation to make your writing easy to read. You use punctuation to aid in reading, and you use punctuation to prevent misreading. Always your purpose can be expressed in three words—clarity, clarity, clarity.

Granted, the trend today is toward less punctuation. Granted also that the overuse of punctuation, especially quotation marks and italics, calls unwanted attention to writing.

Nevertheless, don't omit punctuation just to go along with the crowd. And don't omit punctuation just to have a clean-looking page. Those sins of omission don't help readers one bit.

When all is said and done, it is the wise writer who realizes that punctuation is like the traffic officer or the annotations on a musical score. Without the officer's directions, drivers wouldn't know when to go. Without the annotations, musicians wouldn't know how to interpret the music.

Without a doubt, learning how to punctuate properly is not an easy task. But if you succeed, you've also accomplished an even harder task, that of helping readers understand what your meaning is.

Mini-Glossary:
Terms Used in the Book

This mini-glossary contains definitions of terms used in special senses in the book. For definitions of grammatical terms in common use, see a dictionary.

Capitalize. To write as uppercase the first letter of a word.
Clause. A group of words that contains a verb.
Essential sentence element. An element that is necessary to the meaning of the sentence. If you remove an essential

sentence element, you change the meaning of what you are writing.

Nonessential sentence element. An element that is not necessary to the basic meaning of the sentence. If a nonessential sentence element is removed, the basic meaning remains the same.

Phrase. A group of words that does not contain a verb.

Sentence element. A word, phrase, or clause.

Punctuation Purposes

Chapter 1. To Introduce

Punctuation is used to separate an introductory sentence element from the main part of the sentence. The introductory element may be as short as a transitional word or phrase or as long as a complete clause.

Punctuation is also used to introduce a question, a statement, or a series. In addition, punctuation is used in the salutation of a letter and with introductory expressions such as *the following* and *that is*.

Regardless of where used, the purpose of introductory punctuation is to make the reader pause, to say to the reader, "Hey! Something's coming."

Introductory punctuation is the subject of this chapter and these other sections:

1.1 To Mark Off a Transitional Word or Phrase

A transitional word or phrase is sometimes placed at the start of a sentence. The purpose of the transition is to lead into the main sentence element, to provide a brief introduction.

Transition at the start of a sentence.

A comma separates the transition from the rest of the sentence. The comma sounds a signal that the main part of the sentence is coming:

Legally, neither party had the right to solicit campaign funds.

Nevertheless, formations of the gamma-endotoxin are proving successful in the control of several lepidopterous pests.

To summarize, the bulk of the report presents positive expectations.

In this state, science materials are locally adopted by individual school districts.

Anyway, daylight was too far gone to accomplish much else other than placing several rows of sod.

On the other hand, the word *become* has a totally different meaning.

Clearly the winner, the team staged a wild party in the locker room.

Transition following a semicolon.

When the transition follows a semicolon, the transition is punctuated as though it were at the start of the sentence:

Jogging can be too strenuous an exercise if done for too long; in other words, don't overdo it.

Neither the corporation nor its stockholders are well served by a governing process that leaves management in doubt about stockholders' views; of course, the views of others should be considered also.

1.2 To Mark Off an Introductory Clause

Introductory clause at the start of a sentence. Use a comma to separate an introductory clause from the main part of the sentence:

> To obtain reliable information about gypsy moth infestations in forested areas, a three-part survey must be conducted.

> Before launching into these matters, you need to think about planning fieldwork on a day-to-day basis.

> When air is evacuated from the chamber, a suction is applied to the water in the ceramic wells.

> By analyzing the variances, we learned that torque differed with all variables except spindle speed.

Introductory clause in the second half of a compound sentence. An introductory clause in the second half of a compound sentence may be punctuated according to either style shown here. According to the first style, a comma appears before and after the introductory clause. In the second style, a comma appears after the clause:

> Air is pumped into the chamber, and, when air is evacuated from the chamber, a suction is applied to the ceramic wells.

or Air is pumped into the chamber, and when air is evacuated from the chamber, a suction is applied to the ceramic wells.

Introductory clause after a semicolon. An introductory clause after a semicolon is punctuated the same as an introductory clause at the start of a sentence:

The porous ceramic is similar to very fine soil; when placed in contact with moist soil, its pores will be completely filled with water.

For years he lived in New York; although he never tired of the pace of the city, he longed for his hometown of Springfield on many occasions.

Multiple introductory elements. Two introductory clauses joined by *and* are punctuated in this manner:

Because we arrived late and because we had to get up early the next morning, we didn't attend the second seminar.

Multiple introductory elements do not call for additional commas. In the example below, no comma is needed after *safety*:

To crown all, once he had reached safety the turncoat had the audacity to write to the czar to justify his conduct.

1.3 Introductory Elements without Punctuation (General)

No punctuation is needed when the introductory element is short and leads smoothly into the sentence:

For a year she did not leave the house except to go shopping.

At noon all activity stops except for a siesta.

In the following pages we take a closer look at alloy production techniques.

Downwind from the site a large canister exploded.

During the past several years production levels at the Fontana facilities have been hard hit by increasing levels of foreign imports.

At your workplace you must post signs that list safety code requirements.

1.4 Introductory Elements without Punctuation (Legal Matter)

Words such as *resolved* and *whereas* are sometimes used to lead into sentences in legal documents. These documents include contracts, resolutions, and wills. Wherever such a word is used, no following comma is needed:

Whereas the Constitution provides . . .

Whereas Robert W. Medeiros has demonstrated 30 years of exemplary service . . .

Whereas the State Assembly has provided for . . .

Resolved by the House of Representatives . . .

Resolved that the concurrent resolution . . .

Provided by the Washington Board of Trade . . .

1.5 Deciding Whether to Punctuate an Introductory Sentence Element

Deciding whether an introductory sentence element needs punctuation can be tricky. Short introductory elements that flow smoothly into the sentence do not need to be separated by a comma from the main part of the sentence—but questions arise. What is a short introductory element? What is a long one?

To answer those questions and to properly punctuate introductory sentence elements, follow the advice given here:

- You will almost always have to place a comma after a transitional word or phrase. For examples, see section 1.1.
- Always place a comma after an introductory clause, the test for a clause being that it is a group of words that contains a verb. For examples, see section 1.2.
- Always use a comma to prevent misreading. Try deleting the comma from the sentence below and see how easy it is to misread it:

  To summarize, the bulk of the report presents positive expectations.

- Always let the reader know what's going on. If there's any doubt as to whether a comma is necessary to signal the start of the main sentence element, then use a comma. No one is going to criticize you for making the reader's task easier.

1.6 To Introduce a Series

Use of the colon.   A colon can be used to introduce a series:

The briefing document covered issues in four areas: safety, energy, capital formation, and international trade.

Colon not used.   A colon is not used when the series is worked into the sentence in this manner:

The briefing document covered issues in the four areas of safety, energy, capital formation, and international trade.

1.7 To Introduce Another Sentence or Sentences

Use a colon to end one sentence while introducing another sentence or series of sentences:

The staff meeting began 20 minutes late: This may explain why the complete agenda was not covered.

League officials rigidly enforced this rule: Anyone found using drugs would be immediately suspended.

The selection process includes these specific considerations: You have to begin by involving appropriate personnel in the decision-making process. Your next two steps are to research your subject and decide whether a computerized text-editing system is practical and feasible. You also have to decide what you want from a text-editing system. The last steps include talking with vendors, drawing up system specifications, and conducting a formal bidding process.

Cross-reference: For guidance on whether to capitalize a statement after introductory punctuation, see section 1.12.

1.8 To Introduce a Question

Use of the comma.   Use a comma to introduce a question that follows its introductory element:

Committee members wondered, Where does the corporation stand on issues surrounding corporate ethics and international operations?

The viscosity was given as 200, but by what standard?

Use of the dash.   To add emphasis to the question, a dash may be used:

The viscosity was given as 200—but by what standard?

Use of the colon.   A colon is used when a complete sentence leads up to the question:

> Committee members asked this question: Where does the corporation stand on issues surrounding corporate ethics and international operations?

Cross-reference: For guidance on when to capitalize a question after introductory punctuation, see section 1.13.

1.9 To Punctuate *as follows* or *the following*

Use of the colon.   A colon is used after *as follows* or *the following* when either expression comes immediately before what is being introduced:

> Attributes of science include the following: a structured discipline or body of knowledge; a way of acquiring new knowledge; an interesting avenue of personal fulfillment; and a social, economic, and cultural influence.

Colon not used.   A colon is not used after *as follows* or *the following* when either expression is written with an intervening sentence as shown here:

> The abrasive blasting chamber is prepared as follows. Note the safety precaution before step 3.
>   1.   Insert the prepared sample.
>   2.   Close and latch the door.
>   WARNING! DON EAR PROTECTORS.
>   3.   Operate the chamber compressor at 125 PSI.

1.10 To Punctuate Expressions Such as *for example, namely, such as,* and *that is*

Preceding and following punctuation. Introductory expressions such as *for example, namely, such as,* and *that is* are punctuated according to these guidelines: (1) The expression is *preceded* by a comma or no punctuation if the break in continuity is a minor one but by a semicolon or a dash if the break is major; (2) the expression is *followed* by a comma or no punctuation:

> An introductory expression such as *for example* is punctuated according to the guidelines given here.

> Planners should consider any of the various sources of curriculum design, for example, the state framework.

> Planners should consider the various sources of curriculum design; for example, the state framework is very helpful.

> Research was performed for each basic industry, namely, agriculture, manufacturing, mining, and transportation.

> I indexed the major theme of the book—that is, how to help writers organize reports.

Use of dashes or parentheses. The expression and the element it introduces may be enclosed in dashes or parentheses:

> The Sundesert Plant—that is, Project 4198—is planned for Riverside County.

> Other modes of organization (namely, attitude, conceptual scheme, process, and skill or delivery system) are commonly advocated.

Use of the colon. A colon is used where a complete sentence follows an introductory expression:

Community service classes possess certain unique characteristics. That is: Community service classes parallel regular credit programs; community service classes are shorter; community service classes are not for credit; and community service classes are paid for by cost-covering fees.

Avoidance of Latin abbreviations.   Concerning clarity, the abbreviations *i.e.* (*id est*: "that is") and *e.g.* (*exempli gratia*: "for example") should be avoided if at all possible. These are Latin abbreviations and are frequently misused by writers and misunderstood by readers.

1.11 To Punctuate the Salutation of a Letter

The salutation of a letter is punctuated with either a comma or a colon. Use a comma for informal situations, situations where you and the reader are on a first-name basis. Use a colon for formal situations such as those frequently encountered in business and government correspondence:

Informal: Dear Patricia,
Formal: Dear Mr. Johnson:

Cross-reference: For the punctuation of a closing of a letter, see section 10.6.

1.12 Capitalization of a Statement after Introductory Punctuation

Capitalization required.   The question often arises as to whether to capitalize a statement that appears after introductory punctuation. The question is answered by adhering to the principle of capitalizing the first letter of a complete sentence that follows a colon:

> The corporation made further progress in the area of equal opportunity employment: During the year the number of minority employees increased by 3 percent, and the number of women employees increased by 6 percent.

Capitalization not required. Do not capitalize the first letter of a list of items that do not make a complete sentence:

> The report focused on five main areas: (1) data relevant to market factors; (2) socioeconomic data; (3) cost factors; (4) institutional constraints; and (5) a statistical review.

1.13 Capitalization of a Question after Introductory Punctuation

The more formal the question, the more usual it is to begin the question with a capital letter:

> The board of directors pondered the question, Why had total expenditures for transportation increased from $33.2 million in 1978 to $49.2 million in 1984?

but Okay, what's the problem here?

Chapter 2. To Separate

The earliest use of punctuation was that of separation. That is, spaces and marks were placed in the writing to separate one idea from the next. The purpose was to give readers a brief chance to take a breath, to collect their wits before moving on.

Over the centuries, writers have devised increasingly varied ways to use language. As the uses of language have grown, so have the uses of punctuation for separation grown and become complex. No longer is punctuation used solely between the main bursts of thought that we call sentences. Now we separate words from words, as in a series of elements or a succession of adjectives before a noun. Now we mark off explanatory elements, and now we separate nonessential ideas from the text around them.

Separation is still separation, however, and here we take on the use of punctuation to separate elements within a sentence.

2.1 Hierarchy of Marks Used for Separation

Within a sentence the marks of separation are the comma, the dash, the parentheses, and the semicolon. These marks establish different degrees of separation according to this hierarchy:

Comma. The comma indicates the least break in continuity.

Dash. The dash establishes a stronger break than that provided by a comma. In addition, the dash is a readily visible device that calls attention to writing.

Parentheses. Parentheses provide a more abrupt break than the comma or the dash.

Cross-reference: For the use of brackets, which provide an abrupt break similar to that provided by parentheses, see section 3.6.

Semicolon. The semicolon is not half of a colon as its name implies. Instead, the semicolon is a cross between a comma and a period. As such, the semicolon provides a greater degree of separation than that established by a comma but less than that established by a period.

At the end of a sentence the marks of separation are the period, the question mark, and the exclamation mark. These marks are dealt with in chapter 10.

2.2 To Mark Off an Interjection

An interjection is a word or phrase inserted into a sentence for emphasis. Commas are used with an interjection:

Perhaps, however, the greatest attraction is the friendliness and hospitality that exemplify Texans everywhere.

At the level of etiquette, then, rules provide reasons for doing one thing rather than another.

Managers, most of all, must be willing to allocate sufficient time and resources.

This, by the way, was not what we expected.

The president's credibility, consequently, was seriously damaged.

2.3 Interjections without Punctuation

When there is no break in continuity and no reason to pause while reading, commas may be omitted from around the interjection:

The crowd was perhaps too hasty in condemning him.

An ad hoc committee is in fact powerless in this situation.

He therefore decided to seize Polish and Swedish possessions on the Baltic coast.

2.4 To Separate for Clarity or Ease of Reading

Use of the comma.   A comma should be used for the sake of clarity in constructions like these:

To Mary, Jones was a hard person to understand.

The morning after, the drunk went away forever.

She recognized the man who entered the room, and gasped.

In 1985, 672 people attended the conference.

A comma should also be used to make the reader's task easier in sentences such as these:

The squad marched in, in single file.

Whatever is, is good.

Comma not used.   No comma is needed in a sentence such as this:

We all recognized that that solution was the wrong one.

2.5 To Separate Adjectives before a Noun

Use of the comma.   A comma is used between coordinate adjectives, that is, adjectives of equal descriptive significance that come before a noun:

Four of them spent the night in a large, cold house.

His remarks carried all the sincerity of a shrewd, scheming politician.

Comma not used. A comma is not used when the adjectives are not coordinate:

The attacker used a heavy steel pipe.

She took her bath in an old porcelain tub.

Noncoordinate adjectives—the instances in which you do not use a comma—can be spotted in two ways. First, if you insert *and* the result sounds awkward: "a heavy and steel pipe." Second, if you reverse the adjectives, the result again sounds awkward: "a steel heavy pipe."

No comma is used between the final adjective and the noun. As an example, the punctuation of this sentence is wrong: "Four of them spent the night in a large, cold, house." No comma is needed between *cold* and *house*.

Cross-reference: To join adjectives before a noun, see section 6.4.

2.6 To Separate Items in a Series

Use of the comma. In a series of three or more elements, the elements are separated by commas:

Educated, devout, and full of acrimony, he dipped his pen in vinegar and wrote a letter of hate.

The poet called for wine, women, and song.

The method we choose must be accurate, simple enough to be used by anyone in the lab, and reasonably inexpensive.

Argument for use of last serial comma. Some writers do not use the last serial comma, that comma being the one just before the *and* that adds the last element in the series. When that comma is omitted, the punctuation is A, B and C instead of A, B, and C.

Nothing about the use of the last serial comma is mandatory, and it can safely be omitted in the vast majority of cases. Nevertheless, its use provides for greater clarity, and clarity is one of the principal purposes of punctuation. Consequently, the use of the last serial comma is highly recommended.

An example of a sentence in which the last serial comma is needed is the sentence below, which is unclearly written as it stands:

> For supper we had wine, salad, steak, baked potatoes with sour cream and chocolate ice cream.

Baked potatoes and sour cream go together, but chocolate ice cream needs to be set off by itself. One additional comma will do the trick:

> For supper we had wine, salad, steak, baked potatoes with sour cream, and chocolate ice cream.

Comma not used.   Commas are not used when the elements are joined by conjunctions:

> The survey reported on the three basic industries of agriculture and mining and manufacturing.

A comma is not used with the ampersand in a series. Similarly, a comma is not used when an organization's name doesn't call for one.

> Dodd, Mead & Company

> Leather Goods, Plastic and Novelty Workers' Union, International

Use of the semicolon.   Semicolons are often desirable to separate long series elements, and semicolons are usually necessary to separate elements containing commas.

In this first example, the semicolons could be replaced with commas. In the second example, the semicolons are necessary:

These philosophies include an underlying knowledge of learning theories; a view of the society and how learners are served with an assessment of needs; and overall goals and objectives that are consistent with the requirements of education.

Special thanks go to Wilbur R. Moore, Chairman, Riverside Elementary School Curriculum Committee; Mary Johannes, Carbon County Unified School District; and Dorothy Chang, Office of the University Trustees, Springfield.

Numerals or letters in a series. Numerals or letters used to identify elements in a series are placed in parentheses. Commas separate short items; semicolons separate long ones.

Management grouped its reorganization efforts into the areas of (1) chemicals and plastics, (2) ferroalloys, and (3) home and auto products.

In his address, the chairman made these points: (a) More than one half of our clothing is made from fibers issuing from petrochemicals; (b) in housing, all plywood is held together with plastic resins; (c) in serving our health needs, an almost inexhaustible number of pharmaceuticals, biologicals, and medicinals are petrochemical in origin; and (d) in transportation, the tires on almost all vehicles are made from synthetic rubber.

Punctuation with *etc.* Although *etc.* is so vague that its use should be discouraged, some writers will continue to use it, and it should be punctuated as shown here:

We brought nails, screws, nuts, bolts, etc. to the job site.

2.7 To Mark Off Complementary or Contrasting Elements

Use of the comma.   Commas are used to mark off complementary or contrasting elements:

Some critics of business suggested, if they did not openly say so, that the millions of people who come to work each day in corporate offices do their jobs in a kind of moral vacuum.

Such a code of ethics should be a document, written in plain language, that clearly and precisely applies to real situations.

Many environmentalists were pleased, rather than alarmed, at the long list of species on the protected list.

That may explain, but it does not excuse, a violation of the law.

The harder they worked, the more they fell behind.

The more they read the law, the more they became confused.

Punctuation not needed.   No punctuation is used when complementary or contrasting elements are short:

Last but not least.

The more the merrier.

The sooner the better.

2.8 To Punctuate Contrasting Elements Featuring *not*

Elements with the word *not*. Commas are used to mark off contrasting elements that begin with the word *not*:

> Energy concerns, not environmental issues, held the spotlight.

> Permanent employees, not student assistants, receive full fringe benefits.

> Corporate policy must follow government policy, not the other way around.

Elements with *not . . . but* and *not only . . . but also*. Commas are usually used with *not . . . but* elements and *not only . . . but also* elements:

> Rear-end torque increases, not because of engine speed, but because of gear ratio.

> The sample size must be adjusted to survey requirements, not only to provide an adequate sample, but also to establish sampling error.

However, it is acceptable to omit commas from *not . . . but* and *not only . . . but also* elements:

> Rear-end torque increases not because of engine speed but because of gear ratio.

> The sample size must be adjusted to survey requirements not only to provide an adequate sample but also to establish sampling error.

2.9 To Mark Off an Explanatory Element within a Sentence

Sometimes words are inserted into a sentence for the purpose of providing an explanation, and the words cause an interruption in reading.

Slight interruption. If the interruption is slight, commas are used:

It was claimed that the textbook, in its discussion of the theory of evolution, violated the plaintiff's right to free exercise of his religion.

The comparison, it seems to me, emphasizes the importance of building on our past.

The student's attitude, generally speaking, determines what he or she will do autonomously.

Abrupt interruption. If the interruption is abrupt, dashes or parentheses may be used:

The method introduced here—sampling with variable-radius plots—is not intended for use in forested areas smaller than 10 acres.

He rebuked them for their spirit of revolt and even claimed—a new complaint this—that they had tried to murder him, his wife, and his eldest son.

Of the corporation's sales of $5.6 billion, about one third ($1.9 billion) came about because of international operations.

2.10 To Mark Off an Explanatory Element at the End of a Sentence

Slight interruption. When the explanatory element is placed at the end of a sentence, a comma is used to show a slight interruption:

Only one square was left to be filled, the last one.

Keetah had an important decision to make, whether to go outside or stay in the village of her ancestors.

Commas are also used when more than one explanatory item follows the main sentence element:

His fingers were poised over the piano's keys, ready to pounce, like a kitten.

She ran faster, her breath coming in deep gasps, her legs pounding harder onto the pavement.

Ivan's evident piety had made him a kind of saint in their eyes, a demanding, frightening saint who gave orders, fought, punished, but whose brow was free from all stain.

Abrupt interruption. A dash or parentheses may be used when the explanatory element is separated abruptly from the main sentence element:

He was interested in concluding a durable peace that would help deliver to him the young lady of his wishes—beautiful and submissive.

We usually obtain a large excess of eggs—approximately 1 ml of eggs for each of seven trays.

For the smooth tube, the composite coefficients from this scheme were in good agreement (-11.4 to $+6.9$).

Composite coefficients are explained in the appendix on methods (appendix 3).

A colon may be used to provide an abrupt degree of separation:

They needed only one thing: money.

Keetah had an important decision to make: whether to go outside or stay in the village of her ancestors.

Cross-reference: For capitalization after a colon, see sections 1.12 and 1.13.

2.11 To Punctuate a Compound Sentence

Use of the comma. A compound sentence consists of two simple sentences joined by a conjunction such as *and*, *but*, *for*, *or*, *so*, or *yet*. A comma comes before the conjunction:

Reasonable people are beginning to look for perspectives on the question of corporate conduct, for these perspectives are necessary.

Serious cases call for alerts to be reported as quickly as possible, and plant managers should be trained to recognize these cases.

A compound sentence can be made up of three simple sentences separated by commas:

He planned the trip with utmost care, for his itinerary consisted of numerous stops, and everything about the journey went smoothly.

A compound sentence can be written as an imperative, that is, as a direct order or set of instructions. A comma separates the parts of an imperative compound sentence as shown below. The sentence's subject, which is not written in an imperative sentence, is indicated in brackets:

[You] Place the gearshift lever in low, and [you] slowly release the clutch while depressing the gas pedal.

[You] Drop us a line, or [you] give us a call, or [you] come by and see us again.

Comma not used. No comma is needed in a short compound sentence where the elements are closely related:

They laughed and they cried.

Thomas ran and his wife walked to the bus stop.

Use of the semicolon. For a more abrupt break than that provided by a comma, you may use a semicolon to separate the parts of a compound sentence. No conjunction is used:

Instructional goals are general statements that define the desired ends of education; objectives are more specific statements of the steps involved in reaching those goals.

California has several standards covering required medical services; these standards mandate different protective services for different types and sizes of businesses.

2.12 To Punctuate a Sentence with a Compound Predicate

Don't confuse a compound sentence with a compound predicate in a simple sentence. A compound sentence has two or more subjects and predicates. A simple sentence with a compound predicate has one subject with two things being said about it, that is, two predicates.

Use of the comma.   When the parts of a compound predicate are very long, a comma may be used to provide some degree of separation between them:

> McQueen began by denouncing Spake's ungenerosity and unfairness toward Robison, and then proceeded to tear into and demolish Spake's overall character.

> The Khedive Ismail of Egypt had arrived at the crest of his highly prosperous career by the end of the 1860s, and had borrowed and spent his nation into bankruptcy and financial ruin.

Comma not used.   When the parts of a compound predicate are short, no comma is necessary:

> These standards require different protective measures and establish different measurement criteria.

> We are setting up an Economic Evaluation Section and reviewing our long-term investment strategy.

As in many other instances of comma usage, placing a comma before *and* in either of the examples just given would not be wrong. It's just that a comma in those situations simply isn't necessary.

2.13 To Mark Off an Essential Element

An essential element is one that cannot be removed from a sentence without changing the basic meaning of the sentence. An essential element is also called a *restrictive* element because it restricts, limits, defines, or identifies the word or sentence element it refers to. In other words, a restrictive element is essential to the meaning of the sentence. Therefore, we'll use the term *essential* here.

In the example below, note these words: "that flows out of the Vaca Hills."

The creek that flows out of the Vaca Hills is a source of pleasure for rafters.

If "that flows out of the Vaca Hills" is removed, the sentence reads: "The creek is a source of pleasure for rafters." Now we don't know which creek is meant. So that the reader can understand what's being talked about, the element "that flows out of the Vaca Hills" is provided, and it is essential to the meaning of the sentence.

Essential element at the beginning of a sentence.
When an essential element appears at the beginning of a sentence, the element is punctuated like any introductory sentence element. An example can be made of this sentence:

In our business and personal conduct, we must set rigorous standards. (The element at the beginning of the sentence is necessary to define what the standards apply to.)

That example reads smoothly enough so that the comma may be omitted:

In our business and personal conduct we must set rigorous standards.

Otherwise, an essential introductory clause that contains a verb is punctuated with a comma:

If we participate constructively in the policy-making process, we can help obtain responsible legislation. (Without the opening essential element, the second part of the sentence is vague.)

Cross-reference: For more help with punctuating introductory sentence elements, see sections 1.1 through 1.5.

Essential element at the end of a sentence.

If the essential element is placed at the end of a sentence, a comma is not used:

We must set rigorous standards in our business and personal conduct.

We can help obtain responsible legislation if we participate constructively in the policy-making process.

The young man you see on the ski slopes every weekend is Mary's son Tim. (If Mary has more than one son, his name is essential to the meaning of the sentence.)

Essential element in the middle of a sentence.

An essential element in the middle of a sentence is not marked off with commas:

All steam units that are less than 10 years old should be described in the report. ("That are less than 10 years old" is essential to the meaning of the sentence.)

Vendors who discover problems as part of service work are valuable assets. ("Who discover problems as part of service work" are words essential to the meaning of the sentence.)

Shakespeare's play *Romeo and Juliet* is a tragedy. (Shakespeare wrote more than one play; therefore, the title is essential to the meaning of the sentence.)

2.14 To Mark Off a Nonessential Element

A writer sometimes puts into a sentence an element—a word, phrase, or clause—that adds to the basic meaning of the sentence. This type of element provides descriptive detail useful to the reader. If this element is taken out of the sentence, the basic meaning remains unchanged. A word, phrase, or clause used in this manner is *nonessential*; that is, it is not essential to the basic meaning of the sentence. A nonessential element is also known as a *nonrestrictive* element.

An example of a nonessential element is the clause "which flows out of the Vaca Hills" in the sentence below:

> Cache Creek, which flows out of the Vaca Hills, is a source of pleasure for rafters.

We know what creek the writer is talking about because it is named—Cache Creek. Therefore, the basic meaning of the sentence is this: "Cache Creek is a source of pleasure for rafters." The clause "which flows out of the Vaca Hills" is not essential to the basic meaning of the sentence.

Commas are used to set off nonessential elements whether the elements appear at the beginning of a sentence, in its middle, or at its end.

Nonessential element in the middle of a sentence.
When the nonessential element is placed in the middle of a sentence, the element is preceded and followed by a comma:

> Azevedo's Department Store, which opened only last month, is doing a brisk business. (The clause beginning with "which" provides a description not necessary to the basic meaning of the sentence.)

> Our dog, which was sleeping in the sun in the backyard, paid no attention to the children splashing in the pool. (The clause beginning with "which" provides descriptive detail not necessary to the basic meaning of the sentence.)

> Mary's husband, John, worked overtime every night last week. (Mary has only one husband; his name is not essential in this sentence.)

> The regimental commander, Lieutenant Colonel Roosevelt, ordered the charge. (A regiment has only one commander; his name is not necessary to the basic meaning of the sentence.)

Nonessential element at the end of a sentence.

When a nonessential element appears at the end of a sentence, a comma is used as shown in these examples:

The man who worked overtime every night last week was Mary's husband, John.

The charge was ordered by Lieutenant Colonel Roosevelt, the regimental commander.

We wish to make our own decisions about which products to use, as long as we are fully informed of the risks involved.

We must serve to right racial wrongs, if we can serve at all.

Nonessential elements at the beginning of a sentence.

In the two examples just given, the nonessential elements read like afterthoughts. If these elements were placed at the front of the sentence, a comma would be used in this manner:

As long as we are fully informed of the risks involved, we wish to make our own decisions about which products to use.

If we can serve at all, we must serve to right racial wrongs.

Cross-reference: The punctuation of introductory sentence elements is covered in greater detail in sections 1.1 through 1.5.

2.15 Essential and Nonessential Elements and *that*, *which*, and *who*

Essential and nonessential elements are introduced with the words *that*, *which*, or *who*, depending upon the situations described here.

Use of *that*.

That is used to introduce an essential element that refers to an inanimate object or an animal without a name. No comma is used:

The training that our organization gives is free.

This section contains worksheets that community planners may use when evaluating programs.

Performance that is measured on college entrance exams is used as an indicator of the general level of learning.

National Park Service representatives said their number one problem consisted of grizzly bears that mauled hikers in Glacier and Yellowstone National Parks.

Use of *which*.

Which is used to introduce a nonessential clause that refers to an inanimate object or an animal without a name. Commas are used because the elements are nonessential:

A one-mile run is grueling but not at all like the World Series, which lasts seven days.

Specificity of training, which is a bedrock of modern athletics, means that you concentrate your training in the event you're competing in.

Four Chinese alligators, which were the first ever to hatch in a zoo, emerged from their eggs in August.

Which occasionally may be used with essential elements to avoid the unwanted repetition of *that*:

He said that the training which our organization gives is free.

Use of *who*. *Who* is used when an essential or nonessential element refers to a human being or an animal with a name. Commas are not used with essential items but are used with nonessential items:

Officials punished the people of Alta California who did not want to trade with Spanish ships.

Dr. Groves, who will perform the surgery, said that Brian has an excellent chance for full recovery.

Best Kitten Award at the show went to Quidalia Pluribus, who won handily.

2.16 Punctuation with Combined Sentence Types

The principles of punctuation remain the same when you start combining sentence types.

As an example, when you place an introductory clause in front of a compound sentence, the punctuation is:

If something had ever been possible between them, the time for it had passed long ago, and they no longer wrote or called each other.

When you place a nonessential element inside part of a compound sentence, the punctuation is:

She couldn't get up her nerve, which was never fiery, to protest, but she was able to take revenge in her own way.

When you place an explanatory element at the end of a compound sentence, the punctuation is:

We ate quail at leisure, and we peered through the blind, listening to the geese make small talk in the distance.

All sorts of combinations are possible, but your reader will best understand you if you write short, uncomplicated sentences.

2.17 Spacing

Spacing is a form of punctuation, and the spacing requirements given here are standard for typewritten work.

Vertical spacing. Double-space drafts, school papers, and manuscripts submitted for publication. Single-space letters and memos.

Horizontal spacing. Begin a new paragraph by indenting five spaces from the left margin. After a sentence's ending punctuation leave two spaces. Leave two spaces after a colon, except that no spacing is placed on either side of a colon in scriptural references (Ruth 3:2-5), with hours and minutes (10:18 p.m.), and with volume and page numbers (1:14-17).

After a comma or semicolon leave one space. Before or after a dash or hyphen leave no space.

Before an opening (initial) parenthesis or bracket, leave one space. Between the opening parenthesis or bracket and the first letter following, leave no space. Before a closing parenthesis or bracket, leave no space. After a closing parenthesis or bracket, (1) leave no space before any following punctuation, or (2) leave one space before the first letter following.

Spacing with initials and abbreviations. Use single spacing between the periods and initials of a person's name (J. W. Meflin).

Use no spacing between the periods and letters of initials of an organization (U.S. Steel), if that is the organization's style.

However, the punctuation of abbreviations is somewhat simplified these days, for many abbreviations are now written without internal periods. As an example, the American Medical Association can be abbreviated as AMA, not A.M.A.

Exceptions: In a few cases, spacing requirements vary from the ones given here. These exceptions are covered in the sections that pertain to those particular usages.

Chapter 3. To Punctuate Quotations and Dialogue

A quotation is a passage copied from the work of another writer. Dialogue is talk between two or more people. Even though the principles for punctuating them are similar, don't confuse the two. Quotations are copied language. Dialogue is original language.

Regardless of the similarities and differences, both require the writer to have an accurate knowledge of how to use quotation marks and related punctuation—the subjects of this chapter.

3.1 Run-in or Block-indented?

One way to incorporate a quotation into text is to write it as part of the text itself. A quotation used in this manner is called a *run-in quotation*. Quotation marks are placed around a run-in quotation.

Another way is to set the quotation off from the text by indenting it five spaces from both left and right margins and by providing double the usual spacing above and below the quotation. Quotation marks are not placed around a block-indented quotation. Block-indented quotations are also called *block quotations*, *excerpts*, and *extracts*.

The decision whether to run in a quotation or block indent it can be based primarily on the rough guideline of length. Generally speaking, a short quotation, one of fewer than five to eight typed lines, can be run in, while anything longer can be block indented.

Besides counting lines, you should also consider these factors:

1. Purpose of the quotation. If you are comparing quotations, they should all be set off from the text regardless of length.

2. Nature of what you're writing. Newspaper style rarely uses block-indented quotations, some scholarly works use block indentation heavily, and poetry is quoted according to separate rules of its own (see 3.9).

3.2 Introductory Punctuation with Quotations

Use of the comma. A comma is frequently used as the introductory mark with short quotations and following words such as *say, said, writes, wrote,* and *remarked.*

> Churchill wrote, "To jaw-jaw is better than to war-war."

> As Churchill remarked, "To jaw-jaw is better than to war-war."

An intervening statement after *said* or similar words does not eliminate the need for the introductory comma:

> Walter Cronkite said when signing off, "And that's the way it is."

A broken quotation takes commas in this manner:

> "And," as Cronkite says, "that's the way it is."

Comma not used. No comma is needed if the quotation is worked smoothly into the sentence:

> Churchill says that "to jaw-jaw is better than to war-war."

> The terse message was "Sighted sub, sank same."

Use of the colon. A colon can be used as the introductory mark with a statement, regardless of length, made by a prominent person. In this regard, the colon replaces the introductory comma, and the use of the colon is reserved for writing of a more formal or scholarly nature:

Churchill wrote: "To jaw-jaw is better than to war-war."

A block-indented quotation can be introduced with a colon:

> In *The Sea Around Us,* Rachel Carson provides this sensitive interpretation of her subject:
>
> The sea lies all about us. The commerce of all lands must cross it. The very winds that move over the lands have been cradled on its broad expanse and seek ever to return to it. The continents themselves dissolve and pass to the sea, in grain after grain of eroded land. So the rains that rose from it return again in rivers.

Colon not used. When the introductory sentence leads directly into a block-indented quotation, a colon is not used:

> In an impassioned statement on the duties of a writer, William Faulkner said that a writer's only responsibility
>
> is to his art. He will be completely ruthless if he is a good one. He has a dream. It anguishes him so much he must get rid of it. He has no peace until then. Everything goes by the board: honor, pride, decency, security, happiness, all, to get the book written. If a writer has to rob his mother, he will not hesitate; the "Ode on a Grecian Urn" is worth any number of old ladies.

3.3 Double Marks or Single?

Quoted words, phrases, or sentences run into text are enclosed in double quotation marks. Single quotation marks enclose quotations within run-in quotations; double marks are used for quotations within these; and so on:

> "I was given a tour of Chapel Hill," he explained, "and I was taken through the plant. I left the place and

said to myself, 'What a great place to work. This is life. Accomplishment. Challenges.' Then the reality hit me and I called home and told my wife, 'Start packing. We're moving.' "

The speaker began by saying, "I want to tell you a story about a little girl. This little girl said, 'My favorite poem is "The Raven." I read it every night.' "

Material set off from the text as a block-indented quotation is not enclosed in quotation marks. However, quoted matter within a block quotation is enclosed in double quotation marks, even if the source quoted used single marks.

An example can be made of the passage below, which is from Margaret Craven's novel *I Heard the Owl Call My Name.* In the original, the bishop is speaking to a vicar, and the quotation marks are used thus:

> "It is an old village—nobody knows how old. According to the myth, after the great flood two brothers were the only human beings left alive in the world, and they heard a voice speak and it said, 'Come, Wolf, lend them your skin that they may go fleetly and find themselves a home.' And in the wolf's skin the brothers moved south until they came to a small and lovely valley on a river's edge."

If you block indented that quotation, the opening double quote would drop off, and the interior single quote would be doubled. With an appropriate introductory statement, the passage would appear like this:

The young vicar remembered what his bishop had told him of the village:

> It is an old village—nobody knows how old. According to the myth, after the great flood two brothers were the only human beings left alive in the world, and they heard a voice speak and it said, "Come, Wolf, lend them your skin that they may go fleetly and find them-

selves a home.'' And in the wolf's skin the brothers moved south until they came to a small and lovely valley on a river's edge.

3.4 Capitalization of Quotations

Capitalization required. Capitalize the first letter of a complete quoted sentence, regardless of length:

As Yogi Berra is credited with saying, ''It isn't over till it's over.''

As Alexandr Solzhenitsyn wrote in *The Gulag Archipelago*:

The Kolyma was the greatest and most famous island, the pole of ferocity of that amazing country of *Gulag* which, though scattered in an Archipelago geographically, was, in the psychological sense, fused into a continent—an almost invisible, almost imperceptible country inhabited by the zek people.

Capitalization not required. A sentence fragment worked into the text does not begin with a capital letter:

The chairwoman reported that ''these safety procedures worked'' because of the skills and dedication of employees.

Similarly, a block-indented quotation that does not begin with a complete sentence also does not begin with a capital letter:

In *The Gulag Archipelago*, Alexandr Solzhenitsyn wrote that the Kolyma

was the greatest and most famous island, the pole of ferocity.

Changes to initial capitalization. A
quotation worked smoothly into the sentence and not preceded by introductory punctuation does not begin with a capital letter even though the original was capitalized:

> Yogi Berra is credited with saying that "it isn't over till it's over."

Similarly, a lowercase letter in the original may be capitalized when quoted and when the structure of the text suggests it. Note this sentence from Aldo Leopold's *A Sand County Almanac*:

> For us of the minority, the opportunity to see geese is more important than television, and the chance to find a pasque-flower is a right as inalienable as free speech.

A major portion of that sentence can be quoted this way:

> Aldo Leopold wrote, "The opportunity to see geese is more important than television, and the chance to find a pasque-flower is a right as inalienable as free speech."

In legal works and in some scholarly writing, a change in capitalization is shown in brackets:

> Civil Code section 41583.5 requires a homeowner "[t]o be liable for such instances of neglect or malfeasance."

Changes to internal capitalization.
Internal capitalization should not be changed except following ellipsis points. See section 3.7.

3.5 Punctuating Silent Changes to Quotations

When you quote a passage, you must reproduce exactly the wording, spelling, capitalization, and punctuation of the original. Despite the strict sound of that sentence, a few changes are permitted.

One category of changes consists of those that are silent, that is, changes that are not obvious to the reader. These changes are dealt with here. Obvious changes are covered in section 3.6.

Permissible silent changes are:

1. Single quotation marks may be changed to double and double to single (see 3.3).
2. The initial letter may be changed from a capital letter to a lowercase one or from lowercase to capital (see 3.4).
3. Internal capitalization may be changed (see 3.7).
4. Final punctuation may be changed (see 3.19).
5. Footnote or source references in the original may be removed, provided you add your own source citations (see 3.15 and chapter 9).
6. An obvious typographical error in a modern work may be silently corrected.
7. Spelling and punctuation in an older work may be modernized. Similarly, British spelling is sometimes changed to American. The reader should be told of such changes, in a preface, in a footnote, or elsewhere.

With reference to items 6 and 7, defining what is modern and what is old is difficult business. The difficulty arises because language changes slowly, unevenly, and not according to the calendar.

Nevertheless, some help can be had from a brief history lesson. Before approximately 1800, many people spelled according to whim or personal taste. Since then, spelling has become more and more standardized, although it certainly isn't to everyone's liking. Consequently, works written since about 1850 generally use the same pattern of spelling as used today.

As for punctuation, it has changed little during the last century, except that writers are using fewer and fewer marks.

3.6 Punctuating Obvious Changes to Quotations

Use of brackets.   Obvious changes to quotations are made by using square brackets, not parentheses. The brackets can enclose interpretations, corrections, explanations, or comments:

> "She'd never seen him [Bogie] with a woman who didn't drink."

> "Despite the shelling, Bur[r]ington remained at his post."

> "The current status of technical writers in Australia [as reported by Connolly and Butler] is such that the Australians use the U.K. system."

> "One study suggests four stages for screening: list generation, initial selection, intermediate selection, and final selection. [See the paper by Stelma and Ing, presented later. —Editor]. That same study proposes the establishment of an expanded priority ranking."

Contempt, scorn, or doubt may sometimes be shown by [!] or [?]. The reader is better served, however, by written explanations than by the vague use of punctuation.

Emphasis added.   If you wish to add emphasis to a word or words being quoted, underline them; in printed material, the underlining is shown as italics. The next step is to tell the reader that you did indeed add the emphasis. This may be done in the source citation for the quotation, but that citation could be a note or reference at the back of the book and hundreds of pages away from the quotation. All things considered, it is frequently better to mention the added emphasis right at the quotation by using either of the following methods.

You may use parentheses directly after the quotation and outside of the quotation marks:

> "This spurred Spain to secure its old claim to the *empty* land" (emphasis added).

You may use brackets directly after the underlined (italicized) portion and inside the quotation marks:

> "That mistrust is the most *serious* [italics added] obstacle in the way of reducing the burdens caused by regulation."

Emphasis in original.   If you wish to point out that the italics were in the original, you may use parentheses or brackets and expressions such as "italics in original" or "emphasis in original." Better still, give the original author's name.

> "Only *seventeen* of the giant condors are known to be alive" (emphasis in original).

> "A recent cutoff has radically changed the position, and Delta is now *two miles above* [Twain's italics] Vicksburg."

Error in original.   A misspelled word, a word wrongly used, or a grammatical error in the original may be shown by use of the word *sic* (meaning "so" or "thus"). No period comes after *sic,* for it is not an abbreviation but a complete word. Brackets are placed around *sic*; italics or underlining is optional.

A typical use of *sic* is this one:

> "Author's [sic] should get a little recognition for their contributions."

The example just given should read ''authors''—no apostrophe.

No need exists to call attention to every variation or oddity of expression in quoted material. For instance, William Faulkner used a variant spelling of *apologize* in *Light in August*, and it would be sheer nit-picking to insert *sic* into this passage:

> ''I would not mean just that,'' the stranger said. His tone was a little placative. He contrived at once to apologise without surrendering one jot of his conviction.

Words missing in original.   To indicate words missing or illegible in the original, use three blank spaces, with or without brackets. Brackets are also put around missing letters or words inserted into the text:

> In a letter intended for the public at large, Columbus described the land he had discovered on his first voyage: ''This other, Española, has   greater circumference than the whole   Spain from Col[ibre in Catal]unya, by the seacoast, as far   Fuente Ravia in Biscay.

Exception: Newspaper style uses parentheses in place of brackets for the applications described in this section.

3.7 Punctuating Omissions from Quotations

A writer may choose to omit part of a quotation. The omission is the *ellipsis*, and the ellipsis is replaced with *ellipsis points*.

Typing ellipsis points.   Ellipsis points are periods typed on the line, with one space between each period. A single space separates text or punctuation from the first ellipsis point, and a single space separates the final ellipsis point from the resumption of the text.

Do not use asterisks in place of ellipsis points.

Ellipsis points to replace part of a
sentence. Three ellipsis points are used to replace part of a sentence. Adjacent punctuation may be retained if doing so helps retain the meaning of the original. In the sentence below, reprinted here in its entirety, note the comma after "princes":

> Dazzled by these "splendidly mounted princes," as *The Times* called them, few observers had eyes for the ninth king, the only one among them who was to achieve greatness as a man.
>   (Barbara W. Tuchman, *The Guns of August*)

That sentence can be quoted and shortened in this manner, with no comma after "princes":

> Dazzled by these "splendidly mounted princes" . . . few observers had eyes for the ninth king, the only one among them who was to achieve greatness as a man.

If the comma after "princes" is retained, it should be kept inside the ending quotation mark, the same place it was in the original:

> Dazzled by these "splendidly mounted princes," . . . few observers had eyes for the ninth king, the only one among them who was to achieve greatness as a man.

Ellipsis points to replace a sentence
or sentences. Three ellipsis points may be used to show the omission of a sentence or sentences. For purposes of comparison, we'll continue with this passage from Tuchman's *The Guns of August*. In its entirety the passage reads:

> Dazzled by these "splendidly mounted princes," as *The Times* called them, few observers had eyes for the ninth king, the only one among them who was to achieve greatness as a man. Despite his great height and

perfect horsemanship, Albert, King of the Belgians, who disliked the pomp of royal ceremony, contrived in that company to look both embarrassed and absent-minded. He was then thirty-five and had been on the throne barely a year.

The second sentence could be removed and replaced with three ellipsis points:

Dazzled by these ''splendidly mounted princes,'' as *The Times* called them, few observers had eyes for the ninth king, the only one among them who was to achieve greatness as a man . . . He was then thirty-five and had been on the throne barely a year.

When omitting a sentence or sentences, the use of three ellipsis points without ending punctuation is the simplest technique but not the most precise. A more precise technique is to retain a sentence's ending punctuation—period, question mark, or exclamation mark—and place three ellipsis points after the ending punctuation. Notice the use of the period and ellipsis points after ''man'' in the example below. No space appears between ''man'' and the period, as is standard with ending punctuation. A single space appears between the period and the first ellipsis point and between each ellipsis point. Two spaces appear between the final ellipsis point and the resumption of text.

Dazzled by these ''splendidly mounted princes'' . . . few observers had eyes for the ninth king, the only one among them who was to achieve greatness as a man. . . . He was then thirty-five and had been on the throne for barely a year.

If you ended the first sentence after ''king,'' there would be no need to retain the comma that appears there. You could use a period and three points, or you could simply use three points:

Dazzled by these "splendidly mounted princes" . . . few observers had eyes for the ninth king. . . . He was then thirty-five and had been on the throne for barely a year.

or Dazzled by these "splendidly mounted princes" . . . few observers had eyes for the ninth king . . . He was then thirty-five and had been on the throne for barely a year.

It is usually better to retain a sentence's ending punctuation and add three ellipsis points than to just use the three points. The first method allows keeping the flavor of the sentence's ending punctuation, a factor that is important if that punctuation happens to be an exclamation mark or a question mark. And, of course, whichever method you choose, you should stick to it throughout the manuscript.

Ellipsis points in place of lines of poetry. The omission of a line or several consecutive lines of poetry is shown by a line of ellipsis points approximately the length of the line above it.

Ask me no more where Jove bestows,
. . . .
For in your beauty's orient deep
These flowers, as in their causes, sleep.

(Thomas Carew, "Song")

Ellipsis points not needed. Ellipsis points are not needed at the beginning or end of a quoted passage. That statement holds true whether the quoted passage is a sentence fragment, a complete sentence, or more, and whether the quotation is run in or block indented. The rationale is that unless you are quoting the first or last sentence of a work, something comes before and something follows what is quoted, and readers are well aware of that fact.

As an example, the following passage is based on lines

from Jeremy Campbell's *Grammatical Man*. No beginning and ending ellipsis points are used around the quoted portions:

> Complexity is "made possible by redundancy and generated by rules." Rules are a form of "stored information." It is safe to say that "the power of a small number of fixed rules to produce an *unpredictable* amount of complexity is very striking."

Exception: Ending ellipsis points should be used when the thought of the passage is incomplete:

> If women had wives to keep house for them, to stay home with vomiting children, to get the car fixed, fight with the painters . . .
>
> (Gail Sheehy, *Passages*)

Capitalization following ellipsis points.

A lowercase letter in the original may be changed to a capital letter when quoted if it indicates that a new sentence is beginning.

This principle can be demonstrated by using the following passage, in its entirety, from Daniel J. Boorstin's *The Discoverers*:

> He did not make his living by astronomy or by any application of astronomy. By our standards, at least, he was wonderfully versatile, which put him in the mainstream of the High Renaissance.

The word "he" in the last sentence may be capitalized when the passage is quoted thus:

> He did not make his living by astronomy or by any application of astronomy. . . . He was wonderfully versatile, which put him in the mainstream of the High Renaissance.

3.8 Quotation Marks with More Than One Paragraph

Not block-indented. Newspaper and magazine styles do not always allow for the use of block-indented quotes. In such a style, if a quotation runs more than one paragraph, the quotation marks are used in this manner: (1) Place quotation marks at the start of each paragraph, and (2) do not place quotation marks at the end of any paragraph except the last one:

> "The earthfill was leveled by using conventional techniques. The fill was then tamped, packed, and rolled. A heat source was placed on top of the earthfill, and the cables that carried power to the heat source were sunk about one inch into the earthfill.
>
> "A plastic film was placed over the earthfill and the heating cables. The purpose of the plastic film is to act as a moisture barrier.
>
> "The total floor area was then divided into four sections of 10 feet by 20 feet each. A nontest section at each end of the plot provided similar conditions."

Block-indented. When a quotation of several paragraphs is block indented, the first line of the first paragraph is usually not given any additional indentation. Subsequent paragraphs are given additional indentation:

> The earthfill was leveled by using conventional techniques. The fill was then tamped, packed, and rolled. A heat source was placed on top of the earthfill, and the cables that carried power to the heat source were sunk about one inch into the earthfill.
>
> A plastic film was placed over the earthfill and the heating cables. The purpose of the plastic film is to act as a moisture barrier.
>
> The total floor area was then divided into four sections of 10 feet by 20 feet each. A nontest section at each end of the plot provided similar conditions.

3.9 Punctuating Quotations of Poetry

Run-in quotations.   A line or two of quoted poetry may be run into the text. When so done, the end of a line of poetry is marked by the slant bar (/), with one space on either side of the bar. A colon is used for an introduction that reads abruptly; a comma or no punctuation will work for a smooth lead into the quoted lines. Quotation marks enclose the quoted lines:

> Robert Herrick's "To the Virgins, to Make Much of Time" begins with these words: "Gather ye Rose-buds while ye may, / Old Time is still a flying."

> As Herrick wrote, "Gather ye Rose-buds while ye may, / Old Time is still a flying."

> Herrick advises us to "Gather ye Rose-buds while ye may, / Old Time is still a flying."

Indented quotations.   When more than two lines of poetry are quoted, the quotation is set off from the text. A colon is used as the introductory mark of punctuation, and extra spacing is used above and below the quotation. The portion quoted is centered on the page. Alignment of lines should be reproduced as closely as possible:

> Thou sorrow, venom elf;
> Is this thy play,
> To spin a web out of thyself
> To catch a fly?
> For why?
> (Edward Taylor, "Upon a Spider Catching a Fly")

If lines are too long to be centered on a page, as in Edgar Allan Poe's "The Raven," the quotation should be indented from the left margin and the long lines brought down and also indented:

> Then, methought, the air grew denser, perfumed from
>   an unseen censer
> Swung by seraphim whose footfalls tinkled on the tufted
>   floor.
> "Wretch," I cried, "the God hath lent thee—by these
>   angels he hath sent thee."

Indentation of quoted poetry should be uniform throughout the manuscript. That is, if one quotation of poetry is centered, then all should be centered. If one quotation is too long to be centered and is therefore indented from the left margin, then all quotations of poetry should be indented the same amount.

Quotation marks are not used with block-indented poetry unless the marks are part of the poem itself. Quotation marks at the beginning of a line of poetry are aligned with the first letter of the line above:

> He holds him with his skinny hand,
> "There was a ship," quoth he.
> "Hold off! unhand me, grey-beard loon!"
> Eftsoons his hand dropt he.
>
> > (Samuel Taylor Coleridge,
> > *The Rime of the Ancient Mariner*)

3.10 Quotation Marks with *no* and *yes*

The words *no* and *yes* are not placed in quotation marks unless part of dialogue or a direct quotation:

> Every time I was asked that question my answer was no.
>
> She wanted him to say yes in the worst way.

but   "No," he replied. "I'm just too busy."

> Father was an easy mark: To each of our requests he grinned and said, "Yes."

3.11 Quotation Marks and Rhetorical Questions

Quotation marks are not used with a rhetorical question, a question to which a reply is not expected and often is not possible:

At this point we must pause and ask, What is the fate of society?

But if the question is phrased as direct speech or dialogue, quotation marks are used:

The speaker looked at his audience and asked, "What is the fate of society?"

3.12 Punctuation with Interviews, Lines in a Script, Speeches, or Testimony

When punctuating interviews, lines in a script, speeches, or testimony, quotation marks are not placed around the words spoken. The introductory punctuation can be a colon, a period, or a period and a dash:

Dodge: (*yelling off left*) Tilden!
Halie's voice: Dodge, what are you trying to do?
Dodge: (*yelling off left*) Tilden, get in here!
        (Sam Shepard, *Buried Child*)

Mr. Chairman, Distinguished Guests:
I thank you very much for inviting me to be with you today, for it is indeed a privilege to appear before your organization.

Q. What is your name, rank, and present station?

A. Arthur R. Canby, Colonel, Fort Leonard Wood, Missouri.

Q.—What is your name, rank, and present station?

A.—Arthur R. Canby, Colonel, Fort Leonard Wood, Missouri.

3.13 Punctuation with Display Quotations

Quotation marks are not used with display quotations. A display quotation is primarily an ornament and not part of the text. One example of a display quotation is the epigraph placed at the front of a book. Another example of a display quotation is the quote placed at the start of a chapter.

The source of a display quotation is given on a line following the quotation. Parentheses and brackets are not used. The usual source information consists of the author's name (or only last name if the author is well known) and title of the work. Page number and complete bibliographical information are neither necessary nor desirable.

Source citations should not be given with epigraphs, but explaining the source or commenting on the epigraph can be done in the preface. A display quotation at the start of a chapter sometimes comes with a footnote number.

A typical display quotation looks like this:

The most beautiful thing we can experience is the mysterious. It is the source of all true art and science.
                                    —Albert Einstein, *What I Believe*

3.14 Indirect Speech and Quotation Marks

Quotation marks are not used with indirect speech:

Edward said to Mary that their time was running out.

Don't ask why anymore.

This article tells you how to do it.

If the remarks are changed to direct speech, quotation marks are used:

Edward whispered to Mary, "I'm afraid our time is running out."

Again the chairperson asked, "Why?"

The author said, "I will tell you how to do it."

3.15 Parenthetical References and Quotations

When you use a quotation, you should give credit to your source. One way to do so is to place a parenthetical reference directly after the quotation.

Style of reference—prose.   In its simplest form, a parenthetical reference consists of author and title of work placed inside parentheses and outside the quotation marks. The period comes after the ending parentheses:

"Abstract words such as glory, honor, courage, or hallow were obscene" (Ernest Hemingway, *A Farewell to Arms*).

If full bibliographic information is provided, brackets enclose place and name of publisher and date of publication, as shown below. The abbreviations *p.* or *pp.* are not necessary:

"Abstract words such as glory, honor, courage, or hallow were obscene" (Ernest Hemingway, *A Farewell to Arms* [New York: Charles Scribner's Sons, 1957], 178).

Style of reference—poetry and plays.

References for poetry and plays do not use page number but instead cite divisions such as act, scene, verse, canto, and line. To save space, these terms are not spelled out; instead the reader is often informed in a note such as this:

References are to act, scene, and line. ·

Otherwise, the writing of the parenthetical reference˙is pretty much the same:

Their candles are all out. Take thee that too.
A heavy summons lies like lead upon me,
And yet I would not sleep. Merciful powers,
Restrain in me the cursed thoughts that nature
Gives way to in repose!
(Shakespeare, *The Tragedy of Macbeth* [New York: Washington Square Press, 1959], II. i. 7-11)

The play's divisions are separated by periods, not commas. Arabic numerals may be substituted for roman. No period is necessary at the end of a parenthetical reference after a block quotation, as above.

Subsequent references.

In writing subsequent references, use the author's last name, short title, and page or division number:

(Hemingway, *Farewell to Arms*, 205)

(Shakespeare, *Macbeth*, IV. i. 80-85)

Multiple ending punctuation.

In some cases an exclamation mark or a question mark ends the quotation. That mark must be retained, and the ending punctuation becomes as shown:

"Hell is—other people!" (Jean Paul Sartre, *In Camera*).

Cross-reference: Excessive parenthetical citation clutters the page and proves bothersome to readers. Therefore, it is often wiser to use another method of referring to sources, as explained in chapter 9.

3.16 Punctuating Dialogue

Dialogue is talk between two or more people. In most cases, a separate paragraph is reserved for each speaker. Quotation marks enclose the words spoken:

> His basso voice proclaimed, "There it is, Peter—the wildest, weirdest airplane ever built."
> "Sure," Peter replied cynically, "and you expect me to fly it."

> The doctor told the bishop, "He has three years to live, but doesn't know it."
> The bishop replied, "I'll tell him, but not yet."

In some nonfiction, paragraphing is based on organization of the thought, and one paragraph can contain the dialogue of two or more speakers:

> He was a strange man. I asked him, "Why do you persist so doggedly in searching when clearly one thing after another has failed?" He answered, "I haven't been able to connect properly with life." He nodded slowly in affirmation, like a little boy being questioned by his father.

3.17 Punctuating Interrupted or Faltering Speech

When we talk, our words seldom flow smoothly, without a break for one reason or another. Other people interrupt us, or we hesitate as we search for the right words.

Modern writers recognize this and have devised techniques

to show interrupted or faltering speech. Little about these techniques is standardized, but it should be. Accordingly, what is recommended here is based on the characteristics of punctuation marks themselves and the practices of many of the better writers.

1. Interrupted speech should be shown with a dash (two hyphens on a typewriter) because the dash signifies an abrupt break.
2. Faltering and hesitant speech should be shown with three ellipsis points (three periods with a space between each). The ellipsis points show some break in continuity, but not as large a break as that shown by a dash.

Interrupted speech.
The use of these techniques is aptly demonstrated in a scene from Alison Lurie's novel *Foreign Affairs*. The scene is set in a restaurant, and the speakers are irritated with each other. Because of their irritation, they interrupt each other's talk. Notice that the interrupted sentences do not end in a period, for the thoughts are incomplete.

> "Of course it's all your doing," Edwin remarks, breaking off his loving contemplation of the menu. "If you hadn't given that party—"
> "I never meant for Rosemary to take up with Fred," Vinnie laughs, for surely Edwin is teasing. "I never even considered— "
> "The intentional fallacy."

A comma may be used with the dash to separate interrupted speech from the name of the speaker:

> "I simply don't have time to stop on—," Patti started to say, but Marv interrupted her.

Faltering speech.
As the scene in *Foreign Affairs* progresses, Edwin comments on the meal while trying to continue the argument. The attempt to talk about two subjects

at once causes him to pause for words. The pauses are shown with ellipsis points:

> "Oh, I do. I have nothing against Fred *per se* . . . Thank you, that looks delicious." Edwin gives his sole véronique a concupiscent glance, then delicately attacks it. "Mmm. Perfect. . . . And I admit he's beautiful."

If a comma is used to separate the words from the speaker, the comma may be retained:

> "But . . . I really don't know . . . ," said Jane.

Stuttering. Stuttering is shown by the use of hyphens:

> "I've t-t-tried so many times," he stammered.

3.18 Punctuating Interior Monologue

When writing is used to show the thoughts and not the spoken words of people, the technique can be as shown here, with no quotation marks:

> He thought often of his days in India and knew that his adventures would be the stuff from which good stories are made.

> What am I doing here? she wondered.

Another technique is that of interior monologue. With interior monologue, expressions such as "he thought" and "she wondered" are dropped. Italics (underlining in manuscript) are used for the thoughts themselves. Italics help set off the thoughts from the rest of the text, which can consist of dialogue or narrative. In addition, italics emphasize the urgency of what the character is thinking about.

Interior monologue and speech. In-

terior monologue can be inserted into direct speech. Quotation marks are used in the regular manner to mark the spoken words, and parentheses are used to contain the monologue:

> "You'll have your money by Friday, but just stop pushing me. (*If you keep on pushing me, you jerk, you can forget about your money.*) I'll get hold of the bank today."

Direct speech can be inserted into interior monologue. Parentheses and quotation marks enclose the spoken words:

> *What in the world has happened to him?* ("Tom, speak up! I can barely hear you!") *God, this is a horrible connection!* ("Tom, speak up, dammit!")

Interior monologue and narrative.

Interior monologue can be inserted into narrative where no one is talking. Quotation marks and parentheses are not used:

> The left wing came up, and the plane stalled and spun. *Opposite stick and rudder. That's what they said.* He jammed the stick and rudder pedal to their limits, but the spin tightened up, and the horizon whirled in front of his eyes. *Opposite stick and rudder! Why the hell isn't it working?*

Interior monologue inside of sentences. In the examples just given, the interior mono-

logue has been inserted at the end of a sentence. Thoughts do break into sentences, however, and when they do, they can be set off with three ellipsis points (periods with equal spacing between them):

> "I'll call the bank . . . (*Stop pushing me*) . . . today. You'll have your money by Friday . . . (*Or never, if you keep on pushing me*) . . . but stop pushing me."

3.19 Ending Punctuation and Quotation Marks

Commas and periods.   Commas and periods are placed inside ending quotation marks:

See chapter 8, ''The Wonderful Micromachines,'' which covers the subject thoroughly.

''There's always tomorrow,'' Scarlett said. ''I'll think about it tomorrow.''

Everyone grows tired of a speaker who begins every sentence with ''You know.''

He stood and said, ''I will now recite Frost's 'Mending Wall.' ''

''He don't know nothin'.''

Exclamation marks and question marks.   Exclamation marks and question marks go inside quotation marks if part of the original quotation and outside otherwise:

During Whitman's life, the poem that most audiences wanted to hear him read was ''O Captain! My Captain!''

I am totally and completely fed up with insincere jerks who say, ''Have a nice day''!

Tom asked, ''Why will it take so long to debug the machine?''

Why did Rawlings say, ''It gives me a nauseous feeling, because I'm not doing it''?

She stood, trembling before the class, and asked, ''May I be given another poem to recite other than 'Remembrance'?''

Colons, semicolons, and dashes. Colons, semicolons, and dashes are placed outside of ending quotation marks:

The critic gave only one reason for liking Cyndi Lauper's "Time after Time": It has a haunting melody.

The critic gave only one reason for liking Cyndi Lauper's "Time after Time"—it has a haunting melody.

Jack Webb's most famous remark was "Just the facts"; he said it repeatedly in his role of Sergeant Joe Friday.

If quoted matter ends with a colon, semicolon, or dash, those marks are dropped and a period is placed inside the quotation marks. As an example, consider this sentence:

We are beginning to realize that mineral resources took millions of years to form; once they are removed from the earth, no more will be forthcoming for millions of years.

If the first half of that sentence were quoted, the punctuation would be:

I said, "We are beginning to realize that mineral resources took millions of years to form."

Cross-reference: More information on ending punctuation is provided in chapter 10.

Chapter 4. To Punctuate a Vertical List

A list, sometimes called a *tabulation*, is a series taken out of horizontal sentence structure and arranged vertically. Thus the series "apples, oranges, and pears" becomes this:

apples
oranges
pears

Lists are used to display matter in legal documents, to show choices in multiple choice examinations, to present items in highly visible order, to issue instructions in a sequence, to summarize points in an argument, and for other purposes.

The correct preparation of a list requires a knowledge of punctuation, capitalization, and the typographical ornaments used to call attention to items in a list.

4.1 Introductory Punctuation of a List

Use of the colon. A colon is commonly used to introduce a list.

The briefing document covered issues in four areas:

- safety
- energy
- capital formation
- international trade

Colon not used. The colon is not used if you can read directly from the introductory sentence into the list without pausing:

The briefing document covered issues in the four areas of

- health
- energy
- capital formation
- international trade

4.2 Capitalization of a List

Capitalization required. The first letter of each item in a list is capitalized if that item is a complete sentence:

- The modular system is a smaller, self-contained version of the overall system and is planned for use in smaller communities and industries.
- Included in the modular system is another new technology that replaces chlorine for the disinfection of wastewater following secondary treatment.
- Excess phosphorus in effluent causes the heavy growth of undesirable aquatic plants.

Capitalization not required. Sentence fragments in a list need not be capitalized:

The decision-making process has provided for

- using evaluation results
- determining the need for change
- selecting from alternatives
- implementing selected procedures

Need for consistency. If the need arises to capitalize one item in a list because it is a complete sentence, then all items should begin with a capital letter, even those that are not complete sentences.

4.3 Ending and Internal Punctuation of a List

Ending punctuation required.
A complete sentence ends with a period:

- Minerals form the bulk of the earth's crust.
- Minerals are found in hundreds of varieties.
- Minerals may be reusable.
- Minerals are never renewable.

When list items combine to form a complete sentence, the items are separated by semicolons or commas, and a period is placed after the last item on the list:

You will automatically receive an extension provided all the following conditions are met:

1. your federal and state tax years are the same;
2. you have already received an extension for filing your federal income tax return; and
3. a copy of the form granting you an extension on your federal taxes is on file in our department.

If one or more items is a complete sentence, then each item ends with a period:

- Mathematical formulation not sound.
- Observable data missing.
- One compensation function doubled.
- Percent of reductions not determinate; that is, percent of reductions can vary by a factor of 10 depending upon the sensitivity of values selected.

Ending punctuation not required.
Incomplete sentences or sentence elements do not require ending punctuation.

Select the most important soil type from the following:

a. Yolo loam   c. Arken clay loam
b. Hanford loam   d. San Joaquin sandy loam

Internal punctuation. Punctuation inside of list items is the same as punctuation in regular text:

- When world shortages exist, we fall far short of obtaining needed supplies. When surpluses exist, the ''free world'' supply floods our markets.
- Periods of war have created maximum production demands for minerals and metals; in the periods between wars, conditions have generally been unfavorable to recovery from the strain.
- The condition of domestic metal mining (with the possible exception of copper mining) ranges from poor to critical.

4.4 Calling Attention to Items in a List

You can call attention to items in a list by using numerals, letters, or typographical ornaments such as bullets.

Numerals. Numerals are used when the sequence is important or when the items will be referred to later.

Should one of the tires go flat, you can change it safely and quickly by following this procedure:

1. Park the car off the road and on level ground.
2. Place the shift lever in PARK and set the brake.
3. Remove the jack and spare tire from the trunk.
4. Loosen the lug nuts on the affected wheel. Perform this step while the wheel is still on the ground.
5. Install the jack in the slot on the frame . . .

Numerals can also be used in a question-and-answer format:

1. Q. What is a multinational corporation?

    A. A multinational corporation has its headquarters in one country and subsidiaries and affiliates in a number of additional countries.

2. Q. Is Transglobal a multinational corporation?

    A. Yes. Transglobal has its headquarters in the United States, along with production facilities in 11 states. Overseas, we have subsidiaries and affiliates in . . .

Letters.   Letters may be used in place of numerals to indicate a sequence or provide subsequent reference:

According to the procedure, the bookkeeper records

a.   the amount to be debited
b.   the amount to be credited
c.   a complete explanation of the transaction

Punctuation with numerals and letters.   Use a period without parentheses after numerals or letters that call attention to items in a vertical list.

Problems with numerals and letters.
One of the problems with numbered and lettered lists is that they can be misinterpreted as implying a ranking of some kind.

If the ranking does truly exist, the reader should be told so with statements like "The priority is as shown here" or "Steps must be performed in the following order" or "Ten Steps to Better Beauty Care."

If the ranking does not exist, then use an explanatory statement such as "Here are seven examples of such-and-such." When no ranking is meant, you can also use bullets, covered elsewhere in this chapter.

In addition, when sequence is important and when the list is long, numerals should be used, not letters. People are accustomed to counting to 10, not to *J*.

Bullets.

A bullet appears in typeset material as a small, filled-in circle that is larger than a period. On a typewriter, the bullet is made by striking the lowercase *o*. Bullets can be used in place of numerals or letters and when the sequence is not important:

To get started, it's a good idea to set some goals. Ask yourself:

- Are you aiming for overall fitness, or do you just want to train for triathlons?
- How much time and effort can you devote daily, weekly, and monthly?
- How will training affect your family, friends, and job?

A bullet is known as a *typographical ornament*. Other typographical ornaments sometimes used with lists are triangles, squares, and asterisks.

Dashes.

The dash (two hyphens on a typewriter) can be used in place of a bullet:

Figure 1 shows the following cut-and-paste tools:

— rubber cement
— sponge rubber pad
— X-acto knife
— light table

Headings.

One of the easiest ways to call attention to items in a list is simply to use headings.

Catastrophic incidences of air pollution in the middle of the 20th century include:

1930—Fog combined with coal smoke in the heavily industrialized Meuse Valley in Belgium led to 63 deaths.
1948—Killer smog did its dirty work in the small steel town of Donora, Pennsylvania.
1952—Between December 3 and December 10, thick fog, still air, high humidity, and low temperatures held a stagnant mass of coal smoke, fly ash, and sulfur dioxide over London.

Combinations.
Combinations of letters and numerals and typographical ornaments and headings are frequently used quite effectively:

1. *Diversity of programs*. One of the greatest strengths of a community college is its diversity of programs. These may be categorized as:

    a. College parallel programs
    b. Technical and semiprofessional programs
    c. Vocational, or trade, programs

2. *Remedial programs*. A typical community college offers a variety of remedial and developmental services to help undereducated students. These programs and services include:

    a. Pre-freshman English
    b. Pre-freshman mathematics
    c. English as a second language
    d. Developing reading skills

When it comes to using combinations of typographical ornaments, eye appeal is best served if you stick to the general idea of square with square, round with round. As an example, you could introduce the primary set of items with filled-in squares, and the secondary set with hollow squares. You could also use bullets—filled in for the primary items on a list, hollow for the secondary items, as in this example:

- evaluation at interim points should be provided for
  - analyzing collected information
  - interpreting the analysis
- information should be evaluated to determine
  - quality of the school plan
  - means of measuring accomplishment
  - amount of information collected

Ornaments of different colors may also be used, provided the budget can afford colored printing.

4.5 Spacing, Alignment, and Indentation

Spacing and alignment. A list is set off from the text by providing double the usual spacing above and below the list. No additional spacing is provided between elements of the list.

Horizontal spacing and alignment are accomplished according to these instructions:

- Double-space between any typographical ornament and list item.
- When a numeral or letter precedes an item in a list, place a period after the numeral or the letter and two spaces between the period and list item.
- When numerals or letters precede items in a list, the numerals or letters are aligned on their periods as are columns featuring abbreviations:

> 7.   1066 A.D.
> 8.   44 B.C.
> 9.   325 A.D.
> 10.   4 B.C.

Block indentation. Items in a list may be block indented. When block indentation is used, the typographical ornament, or numeral or letter and associated period, is placed five spaces in from the left margin in typewritten material. Two spaces precede the list item, and five spaces separate it from the right margin:

Summary of advantages of internships for students:

- They learn what the job is like, with all of its demands and pressures.
- They learn if they would like that type of work after graduation.
- They learn what courses they should take to prepare themselves better for such work.

If space is limited, block indentation may not be used, and the list may run from margin to margin.

Paragraph indentation.
The first line of a list may be indented as in regular paragraph style:

Ten steps to making better brochures:

1. Read at least a dozen brochures. Keep brochures that come in the mail, that you receive with purchases, and that you pick up at trade shows.
2. Gather your tools. You'll need your basic report, some white paper $8\frac{1}{2} \times 11$ inches, a typewriter, scissors, and cellophane tape.
3. Choose your readership. Describe your audience in terms of prospective customers, other professionals . . .

Hanging indentation.
In hanging indentation, the first line of each item of a list begins at the left margin. Typographical ornaments, letters, or numerals need not be used. Other lines in the same item are given additional indentation:

Darkroom production techniques include a knowledge of:

The process camera. This camera is used for offset photography and is designed to render true images. The process camera is used for preparing illustrations and photographs for offset printing.

Halftone reproduction. Halftone reproduction is used to prepare an original photograph for the offset press.

Line photography. Line photography is a simple darkroom process that consists of copying original black and white illustrations on film.

4.6 Short Items in a List

Short items in a list are generally displayed in two or three columns:

drugs	duodenum	dying
dual careers	duration	dynamics
dualism	dwarfism	dynorphins
ducks	dyads	dysarthia

4.7 Punctuation of a Glossary

A glossary is a list of words, and their definitions, that are beneficial to an understanding of the text. Words to be defined are arranged alphabetically and placed against the left margin. They are separated from their definitions by periods, dashes, or colons. A definition begins with a capital letter and ends with a period. Hanging indentation is used; that is, lines other than the first line of each definition are indented.

Permit to install. Issued to new sources or modifications of existing sources. Upon completion of installation, the source must be eligible for a permit to operate.

Permit to operate. Issued when a source meets all local, state, and federal regulations.

Variance. Issued before April 15, 1977, for sources not in compliance. The variance prescribed a timetable for installation of control equipment.

4.8 Parallelism

The items in a list or a glossary should be parallel. Parallelism is achieved when all the items are alike in grammatical structure.

In this example, the items are not parallel. The first three are sentence fragments, and the last is a complete sentence.

- employs 3,700 personnel in international markets
- operates plants in five major geographical areas of the world
- sends exports to foreign markets
- the company pays its fair share of taxes, here and abroad

To make that list parallel, take the last item, which is a complete sentence, and turn it into a fragment. The list will look like this:

- employs 3,700 personnel in international markets
- operates plants in five major geographical areas of the world
- sends exports to foreign markets
- pays its fair share of taxes, here and abroad

Chapter 5. The Special Treatment of Titles, Names, Words, and Terms

Italics (underlining on a typewriter) or quotation marks are frequently used to assign special treatment to titles, names, words, and terms. The purpose of the special treatment is to single out the expression, to mark it as being different from the rest of the text. In so doing, you make it easier for the reader to understand what you are writing about.

Special treatment of words and terms also is covered in:

5.1 General Principles for Using Titles

The following general principles apply to the titles of printed works and to works in the visual and performing arts. These principles apply when mentioning titles in your writing.

Punctuation. On a book's title page, punctuation is seldom used to separate title from subtitle; the distinction is made by using different type styles and sizes.

Consequently, when mentioning the book in text, punctuation will have to be placed between title and subtitle.

A title page showing this:

The Word
A Look at the Vocabulary of English

becomes this in text:

The Word: A Look at the Vocabulary of English

Old-fashioned titles and subtitles separated by the word *or* usually have a semicolon placed before *or* and a comma after:

The Mustang-Hunters;
or, The Beautiful Amazon of the Hidden Valley

Otherwise, retain any other punctuation found in the title. And do not place any ending punctuation after the title unless ending punctuation is part of the title or the title comes at the end of a sentence.

Capitalization.

Capitalize the first and last word of a title and all other words in it except articles (*a, an, the*); prepositions (words such as *to, in, with, through*); and conjunctions (words such as *for, and, but*).

Capitalize any word that begins the subtitle, even if the word is an article, preposition, or conjunction:

The Way Things Work:
An Illustrated Encyclopedia of Technology

Do not use all capital letters for any word in a title, even if the title page of a book does. However, an acronym such as *ZIP*, for the postal service's address system, should be left in all capital letters.

Hyphenated words in a title are capitalized according to these principles: (1) Always capitalize the first word, and (2) capitalize the second word if it carries the same weight as the first:

How to Bake a First-rate Pie

but   *Chicago Sun-Times*

Omission of articles. When an article (*a, an, the*) is the first word of a title, omit the article rather than write an awkward sentence.

Instead of writing the following, which does not read smoothly:

Bruce Catton's *The Centennial History of the Civil War* consists of three volumes.

drop the opening *The* and write:

Bruce Catton's *Centennial History of the Civil War* consists of three volumes.

Spelling. Retain the original spelling, but change the ampersand (&) to *and* in text. The ampersand may be retained in footnotes and bibliographic references.

5.2 Title of a Book; Names of Parts of a Book

Book titles. Italics are used for the titles of complete documents such as books, booklets, reports, proposals, brochures, pamphlets, and manuals. In this same category are microfilm and microfiche reproductions:

Finely crafted prose can be found in the book *The Lives of a Cell: Notes of a Biology Watcher*.

Master Poems of the English Language is a useful anthology of poetry.

The company wanted to produce an up-to-date version of its report *Transfer of Technology: A Report on an Emerging Issue*.

Chapter titles. Titles of chapters or appendixes are placed in quotation marks:

The chapter "Geology and Ourselves" begins on page 4.

Please refer to appendix A, "Reduced Field Data."

Punctuation not required.   Italics or quotation marks are not used when referring to common items such as preface, foreword, table of contents, glossary, or index:

References to a book's preface seldom appear in the index.

The bibliography is divided into primary and secondary sources.

Cross-reference: The Bible and its books are treated other than described here. See section 5.12.

5.3 Title of a Periodical

A periodical is a magazine, journal, bulletin, newsletter, or newspaper; also counted as a periodical is a section of a newspaper published separately. Titles of periodicals are displayed in italics:

California Living is a regular feature of the *Sunday San Francisco Examiner*.

The magazine *Modern Maturity* carried an interesting article on retirement in the San Juan Islands.

5.4 Titles of Articles, Essays, and Short Stories

Quotation marks are placed around titles of articles, essays, and short stories:

The lead story, "Harbor's Night Cops," was about Jim Kelly.

One of the most frequently anthologized essays is George Orwell's "Shooting an Elephant."

In this same category are papers read at a meeting or printed in a scholarly journal:

That morning, James G. Shaw read his paper "The Language of Crisis."

5.5 Titles of Unpublished Works, Lectures, and Speeches

Quotation marks are used with the titles of theses, dissertations, and unpublished manuscripts:

For the most complete treatment of the subject, see John Thompson's thesis, "The Settlement Geography of the Sacramento–San Joaquin Delta, California."

According to one story, the book we now know as *Catch-22* was a manuscript titled "Catch 18."

Quotation marks are used with the titles of lectures, speeches, and papers read at a meeting:

Dr. Bryan gave the conference's keynote address, "Subliminal Communication Techniques."

Words such as *diary, journal,* or *memorandum* are lowercased and not placed in quotation marks or italics:

In his letter, Lincoln hinted that McClellan had a "case of the slows."

Webster's daughter kept his frayed diary under lock and key.

5.6 Titles of Legal Cases

The title of a legal case is italicized:

This decision was rendered in *Pells v. Brown*.

Note that all three items—plaintiff, *v.* (versus), and defendant—are italicized. This is a change from the older style in which only the names of plaintiff and defendant were italicized.

Later references to the same case may be shortened; italics are retained:

The appellate court again referred to the *Pells* case.

On appeal, *Pells* was cited frequently.

Italics are not used when referring to the person rather than the case:

It was well past noon before Pells testified.

Further examples of legal style can be found in the Harvard Law Review Association's *A Uniform System of Citation*.

5.7 Titles of Movies and Plays

Title of complete work.   Italics are used for the titles of movies and plays:

He firmly announced that he could not stand to see *Gone With the Wind* one more time.

Neil Simon's *California Suite* is a group of one-act plays.

Names of internal parts.   No special treatment, such as italics or quotation marks, is used when referring to items such as:

act 2   scene 4

5.8 Titles of Musical Works

Short musical works.   Quotation marks are placed around the title of a short musical work such as a song:

As he rode he hummed "Snowbird" to himself.

Long musical works.   Italics are used for the titles of long musical works such as operas, oratorios, symphonies, and concertos:

Handel's *Messiah* has become quite a sing-along event.

The concert was very popular, beginning with Bach's *Italian Concerto* and ending with Dvorak's *Symphony from the New World.*

Porgy and Bess is an opera in three acts by George Gershwin.

In a paper in which both long and short musical works are mentioned, italics may be used for all titles.

Punctuation not required.   Many musical works do not have descriptive titles. Instead these works are identified by the name of their form plus a number or a key signature or all three. These titles are not placed in quotation marks and are not italicized:

C-sharp Minor Quartet
Concerto No. 3
Piano Quartet, op. 25

5.9 Titles of Poems

Short poems.   Quotation marks are used around titles of short poems:

He had to memorize Frost's poem "Stopping by Woods on a Snowy Evening."

Long poems.   A long poem, one that could conceivably be published as a book itself, has its title displayed in italics:

Interest in Chaucer's *Canterbury Tales* remains high today.

In a paper in which both short and long poems are mentioned, italics may be used for all titles.

Use of first line.   When a poem is referred to by its first line, the line is placed in quotation marks. In addition, capitalization follows the style of the poem, not the rules of capitalization of titles:

He agreed with Yeats: "That is no country for old men."

5.10 Titles of Paintings and Sculptures

Italics are used for the titles of paintings, sculptures, drawings, and similar works of art:

Leonardo Da Vinci's *Mona Lisa* is probably the most famous portrait ever painted.

Red Petals is a mobile by Alexander Calder.

Rodin is best remembered for his figure *The Thinker*.

5.11 Titles of Radio and Television Series and Programs

Series are italicized; individual programs or episodes are placed in quotation marks:

''On with the Dance'' was a favorite episode in *Upstairs, Downstairs*.

When a regular program does not feature named episodes, quotation marks may be used for the program's title:

The pensioner spent a lot of his time listening to ''Morning Line,'' his favorite talk show.

5.12 The Bible and Its Books

The title of the Bible and the names of its books are capitalized. Neither italics nor quotation marks are used.

His diary was filled with references to the Bible.

The editors were able to reduce the length of Genesis by cutting out a lot of repetition.

Other sacred works are similarly treated:

The Bible, the Koran, and the Talmud are the world's most revered books.

5.13 Titles within Titles

When a title indicated by quotation marks appears within an italicized title, retain the quotation marks. When a title in italics appears within a title enclosed by quotation marks, retain the italics:

"The Raven" and Poe's Symbolism is the title of a book.

His first published article was *"Huckleberry Finn* a Century Later."

When a title indicated by quotation marks falls within a title requiring quotation marks, the rule is that single quotation marks appear within double quotation marks:

The assignment was to write an essay titled "Appreciation of 'The Raven.' "

Before placing an italicized title within another italicized title, either place quotation marks around the included title, or use no quotation marks or italics with the italicized title:

The scholar took two years to finish his book, *Mark Twain and the Writing of* "Huckleberry Finn."

or The scholar took two years to finish his book, *Mark Twain and the Writing of* Huckleberry Finn.

5.14 Names of Vehicles

Italics are used for the names of ships, submarines, spacecraft, and human-made satellites. Italics are not used with the names of cars and trains. In addition, italics are not used with abbreviations such as *SS* or *HMS,* designations of class or make, and names of space programs:

With the purchase of a Cadillac Seville, they felt that they had really arrived.

The space shuttle *Challenger* carried with it the *Westar 6* communications satellite.

Pentagon officials wanted to buy more C-5 Galaxy jets.

The Burlington Zephyr was the world's first mainline train powered by a diesel-electric locomotive.

An aircraft carrier such as the USS *John F. Kennedy* provides the main striking power of the surface fleet.

5.15 Personal Names with *Jr.* or Degrees

In some cases, punctuation is used when a personal name is followed with *Jr.*, a roman numeral, or any degrees, affiliations, or honorifics.

Jr. and Roman numerals.

In some styles a comma is used to separate *Jr.* from the name it follows:

Douglas Fairbanks, Jr., was a movie star.

Note that in the example above *Jr.* is treated as a parenthetical (nonessential) element and has commas on both sides of it.

The style recommended here, however, is to consider *Jr.* as part of the person's name and not use the separating commas:

William Strunk Jr. was coauthor of *The Elements of Style*.

When the separating commas are not used, as in the example just given, care should be taken to avoid misreading. A former governor of California, who did not want to be addressed as ''Junior Governor,'' had his letterhead printed this way:

Edmund G. Brown Jr., Governor

Without the *Jr.*, the separating comma is appropriate:

John Smith, Governor

This same principle applies when the identical name is carried through later generations. That is, no comma is placed between the name and the Roman numeral:

John D. Rockefeller III was associated with his grandfather's business interests.

With sovereigns and popes, no comma is used between the name and the roman numeral:

Pope Clement VII refused to annul the marriage between Henry VIII and Catherine of Aragon.

Degrees, affiliations, or honorifics.   A comma is used between a person's name and any degrees, affiliations, or honorifics:

As an attorney, the president could have signed his name Abraham Lincoln, Esq.

Anthony Barbieri, LL.D., Ph.D., will give the keynote speech.

Do not use *Mr.*, *Mrs.*, or *Dr.* if another title is used. As an example, it is incorrect to write "Dr. Harvey Close, Ed.D." Drop "Dr." or drop "Ed.D."

5.16 Personal Names with Place Names

It is not necessary to use a comma to set off a place of residence from a person's name:

Called in as a consultant was Dr. Raymond Longwell of New York.

Mr. and Mrs. Siemens of Berlin were among the survivors.

But the place name can be treated as nonessential and set off with commas:

According to witnesses, Pedachenko, a citizen of Russia, was last seen in Minneapolis.

Dr. Raymond Longwell, a New York clinician, was called in as a consultant.

A comma is not used when the place is closely identified with the individual:

> T. E. Lawrence is popularly known as Lawrence of Arabia.

> Mary of Burgundy is one of the signers of the Great Privilege, the Magna Carta of the Netherlands.

Cross-reference: For the treatment of names with essential and nonessential elements, see sections 2.13, 2.14, and 2.15.

5.17 Personal Name Not Given

Writers sometimes find it convenient to not give the name of a person. In that case, the technique is to substitute a blank line, usually 10 spaces long, for the name. Alice Walker did this in her novel *The Color Purple*:

> I hear him mutter somethin' to Mr. ———— sitting on the porch. Mr. ———— call his sister. She stay on the porch talking a little while, then she come back in, shaking.

5.18 Names of Genus, Species, and Subspecies

When the Latin names of animals and plants are used, genus, species, and subspecies are shown in italic type. Genus is capitalized; species and subspecies are not:

> One genus of warrior ant is the *Iridomyrmex*, and a species of this group is the *humilis*. When combining terms you would write *Iridomyrmex humilis*.

> The data apply to southern pine, genus *Pinus*, and to the species *palustris*, *taeda*, *echinata*, and *elliottii*.

5.19 To Introduce a Key Term

One way to introduce a key term is to italicize it the first time it is mentioned. Italics are not used in later references:

The term *implementation* implies that the school shares responsibility with its constituents.

Antifreeze is an example of a *petrochemical*. A petrochemical is a chemical made from petroleum or natural gas.

Elasticity is worth considering. Elasticity can be defined as . . .

Some authors, especially those writing in the popular press, present a key term and its definition without using any special punctuation. These authors rely on context—the words around the term presented—to define the term. An example can be found in Alex Haley's *Roots,* where he mentions a *toubob* as a "slave raider":

Kunta knew that those who were taken by the toubob became slaves, and he had overheard grown-ups talking about slaves in Juffure.

Cross-reference: For more on the handling of definitions in text, see sections 2.9 and 2.10.

5.20 To Add Emphasis or Irony

Emphasis.   One way to add emphasis is to take the element you wish to emphasize and use dashes to set it off from the rest of the sentence:

The man or woman who cannot make a moral choice— who cannot forgo deceit and deception in the eagerness to obtain results—must forfeit any claim to a position of trust.

Emphasis may also be added by using italics:

> We are now only 14 cents *below* the average we need from each person to meet our goal.

> "What *exactly* are you doing?" she persisted in asking.

The use of italics to add emphasis should be limited to single words or short expressions. When complete sentences and whole passages are set in italics, the technique is overworked.

Italics are not necessary when the emphasis is added structurally, that is, by writing the passage to achieve the effect of emphasis:

> Our goal is an important one; we are still below it, but now only 14 cents below.

> "I want to know exactly what you are doing," she said. "Not partially, and don't beat around the bush. Tell me exactly."

Cross-reference: Use of the exclamation point to add emphasis is covered in section 10.9.

Irony. Quotation marks may be used to add irony:

> Studs Terkel had to interview many veterans for his book on the "good" war.

> They had to destroy the village in order to "save" it.

In the example just given, the irony would be apparent without the use of quotation marks. This brings up the point that many of the best writers rely on meaning or structure rather than punctuation to add emphasis or irony.

5.21 To Show Pronunciation

The phonetic spelling (pronunciation) of a word is placed after the word and in brackets or parentheses:

The pronunciation of the tool micrometer (my-KRAHM-mett-ur) should not be confused with the measurement of distance (MY-krow-mee-ter).

5.22 To Show Rhyme Schemes

Italics are used to show rhyme schemes; commas separate verses:

The English or Shakespearian sonnet rhymes *abab*, *cdcd*, *efef*, *gg*. The Spenserian variation is *abab*, *bcbc*, *cdcd*, *ee*.

5.23 Use of Expressions Such as *so-called* and *titled*

Quotation marks or italics are normally not used when an expression is introduced with *so-called*, *called*, *named*, *referred to*, *known as*, or similar term:

He was the president's so-called fair-haired boy.

They lived in the so-called lap of luxury.

He insisted on naming his first son John.

Wyatt Earp is known as one of the participants in the gunfight at the OK Corral.

They referred to it as a compact car because it was.

If the context is that of a quotation, then quotation marks are appropriate:

Motor Trend referred to it as a "compact car" because it was.

The words *titled* or *entitled* are usually not necessary when mentioning a title. Instead of writing "We distributed 2,000 copies of the report titled *Toward a Commonsense Energy Policy*," write:

We distributed 2,000 copies of the report *Toward a Commonsense Energy Policy*.

5.24 Punctuation with *O*, *oh*, and *ah*

O is a form of address and is rarely used in modern writing. *Oh* and *ah* are exclamatory in nature.

O is always capitalized, and punctuation is not used to separate it from the expression it comes before. *Oh* and *ah* are capitalized and punctuated according to the examples below:

Virgil said, "O thrice and four times blessed!"

Have mercy, O Lord!

Oh, think what you will of me!

or   Oh! Think what you will of me!

Ah, what a beautiful sight!

As the statue was unveiled I could only think to myself, Ah, what a beautiful sight!

Take that package, my good man, ah, that's the ticket!

Oh, waiter! Come here please!

5.25 Slang

Quotation marks may be used around slang expressions if the expressions are not typical of the style of writing.

For instance, the *New Yorker* magazine would more than likely place quotation marks around "deeks"—street slang for cops—and use the word like this:

Toughs in the streets recognized them as "deeks."

But a street-smart person talking in a script or a novel would say:

"They're deeks. I can tell by the way they walk. They all walk the same."

5.26 Foreign Words and Phrases

The English language is noted for absorbing words from other languages, and many words once considered foreign need no special attention paid to them. Still, when the use of an unfamiliar foreign term is necessary, the term is written in italics.

To secure the best price for his efforts, he turned his work over to a *commissionnaire*.

No need exists to use italics for such common Latin words and abbreviations as:

etc. et al. e.g. passim

The translation of a foreign word or phrase may be placed after the word or phrase and in parentheses or quotation marks:

He talked glowingly of *deliciae humani generis* (the delights of the human race).

He is the *nawab*, the "nabob" or "governor."

5.27 Words as Words; Letters as Letters

Words as words. When you write about a word or a term, place the expression in italics:

Don't use the word *oral* when you're referring to written and not spoken language.

The expression *Have a nice day* seems rather trite at times.

The definition of an italicized word is placed in quotation marks:

Oral means "of the mouth."

Quotation marks may be used in place of italics when the use of spoken or written language is suggested:

In virtually every paragraph, the writer misuses "presently."

Letters as letters. An individual letter or combination of letters is italicized:

Rare is the word that begins with *q* without a *u* following.

In word games, the combination *qu* can have a high point value.

The name of a letter is not shown in italic type:

His playing gave listeners the alpha and omega of Bensky's tone poem.

The coil is wound in the shape of a wye.

Letters may be used to show shapes:

The elderly couple built an A-frame cabin.

Begin by making a V-shaped trough out of foil.

A letter used as a musical note is capitalized. Italics or quotation marks are not used:

Beethoven's Quartet in B-flat Major is in six movements.

The flute is tuned to the key of C.

When a letter is used as a name it is capitalized and not placed in italics or quotation marks:

As a man of mystery, he was known only as Citizen X.

She grew tired of reading her business law textbook where A was constantly suing B, and she mused that L ought to sue O once in a while.

To show spelling.   To show the spelling of a word, place a hyphen between each letter:

In England, the spelling is with a *u*: c-o-l-o-u-r.

5.28 Old Sayings, Mottoes, and Notices

Old sayings.   Quotation marks are used with an old saying, proverb, or similar expression when it is quoted from a printed or spoken source. Quotation marks are not necessary when the expression is one commonly heard and not traceable to an original source:

The catchphrase of Sunday's sermon is "I will sing and give praise, even with my glory" (Psalms 108:1).

He quickly grew weary of the wing commander saying, "When the going gets tough, the tough get going."

As an anarchist she mistakenly embraced the Scottish proverb "Live and let live."

Don't forget to dot your *i*'s and cross your *t*'s.

Cross-references: With respect to the last example, the use of italics with individual letters is covered in sections 5.27 and 5.29.

Mottoes and notices.
The words of mottoes, notices, and signs when used in text are capitalized like titles; italics or quotation marks are not used:

A red sign saying Fire Exit was placed by each door.

As a joke he had his business cards printed to label him as The Artful Dodger.

5.29 Plurals of Italicized Terms

The plurals of italicized titles (sections 5.2, 5.3, and 5.6 through 5.11) and of words as words and letters as letters (section 5.27) are treated according to these rules: (1) The singular form is italicized; (2) the added *s* or *es* is not.

They went out and bought 10 *Chronicle*s and *Times*es.

Don't use too many *and*s in your writing.

An apostrophe helps prevent misreading of the plural form of letters treated as letters:

The computer printout was speckled with *a*'s and *i*'s (rather than *a*s and *i*s).

Omit the apostrophe if meaning is clear without it:

He lectured on the seven Ms of weight control—METHOD, MEANING . . .

Campuses were scenes of unrest during the 1960s.

Because of the popularity of the letters, there are more than 20 AMAs listed in the directory.

5.30 Apostrophe in Place of a Letter (Contraction)

An apostrophe is used in place of a letter when forming a contraction. Familiar contractions are

can't
shouldn't
don't
wouldn't
it's (for "it is," not *its,* the possessive)
o'clock (for "of the clock")

Advertising has given us constructions such as these, which demonstrate another use of the apostrophe in place of a letter.

bread 'n' butter   quick 'n' easy
fish 'n' chips   soup 'n' salad

The apostrophe is not used with these common shortenings:

coon   possum
Danl (not Dan'l)   Sgt. (not Sg't)
Halloween

Cross-reference: For the use of apostrophes with possessives, see chapter 7.

5.31 Comma in Place of a Word (Elliptical Construction)

An elliptical construction is formed when a comma is used in place of a word or words.

Instead of writing "Time has spoiled the many; love has spoiled the few," you could use an elliptical construction this way:

Time has spoiled the many; love, the few.

Some additional examples of elliptical constructions are:

The theme of her thesis was Martin Luther; more precisely, a critical study of his *Table Talk*.

Ten attended the seminar; 15, the luncheon; and 33, the cocktail hour.

5.32 Different Styles and the Special Treatment of Titles, Names, Words, and Terms

Some publications use quotation marks in place of italics when assigning special treatment to titles, names, words, and terms. In addition, many newspapers save typesetting time by not using italics and by restricting the use of quotation marks to direct quotations. Therefore, titles and similar items, as covered in sections 5.1 through 5.31, are sometimes written as these examples show:

He spent a week reading the book ''The Word: A Look at the Vocabulary of English.''

or He spent a week reading the book The Word: A Look at the Vocabulary of English.

The committee delved into appendix A, ''Reduced Field Data.''

or The committee delved into appendix A, Reduced Field Data.

The magazine ''Modern Maturity'' carried an interesting article on retirement in the San Juan Islands.

or The magazine Modern Maturity carried an interesting article on retirement in the San Juan Islands.

"Red Petals" is a mobile by Alexander Calder.

or   Red Petals is a mobile by Alexander Calder.

The term "implementation" implies that . . .

or   The term implementation implies that . . .

You can establish the proper style by reading the publication you're writing for and following its style.

Chapter 6. To Join or Divide Words

Hyphens are used to join words within sentences or to divide a word at the end of a line. Both functions are covered by numerous rules and even more numerous exceptions. Consequently, the advice given here is meant to summarize the most common situations.

For the use of hyphens with numbers, see sections 8.6, 8.8, 8.12, 8.13, 8.15, 8.17, 8.28, and 8.29.

6.1 Hyphens for Clarity

Always use hyphens to improve the clarity of your writing. Each of the examples below could be misread were it not for the use of hyphens in them:

Specifications called for 10-foot-long rods.
He is an old-clothes dealer.
I'll be wearing a light-blue hat.
They sailed on an American-flag ship.
Meals consisted of canned baby-food.
I bought a little-used car.

6.2 Hyphens with Compound Words

A compound word is a word made up of two or more words. Compound words occur in three types: *open*, *hyphenated*, and *close* (or *solid*).

An open compound is a combination of words that make up a single concept but are spelled as separate words. Examples of open compounds are *blood pressure*, *fellow citizen*, and *real estate*.

A hyphenated compound is a combination of words joined

with a hyphen or hyphens. Examples of hyphenated compounds are *forget-me-not*, *hee-haw*, *off-hours*, and *right-of-way*.

A close compound is a combination of two or more words that were originally separate words but are now spelled as one word. A hyphen is not used to join the parts of a close compound. Examples of close compounds are *fainthearted*, *manhandle*, and *stonecutter*.

Compounds usually begin life as open or hyphenated compounds before becoming close compounds. *Fainthearted*, *manhandle*, and *stonecutter* were at one time open or hyphenated compounds; today we close up their parts.

In addition, current compounds are sometimes written in different forms. As an example, *Webster's Ninth New Collegiate Dictionary* records usages that could show up in this sentence: "Because I was feeling so *run-down*, I got caught in a *rundown* at second base."

The moral of all this is that you must check a dictionary, and a recent one, for the hyphenation of compound words.

You should also know that hyphenated compound nouns, unlike adjectives before a noun (section 6.4), are hyphenated wherever they appear. As examples:

He is a manic-depressive.

He was diagnosed as being a manic-depressive schizophrenic.

Dreyfuss served as a go-between.

Checkpoint Charlie was a go-between meeting point.

The wardrobe people wanted to try the lights on her stand-in.

Other frequently seen compounds are listed in the sections that follow.

In-laws and great-relatives.   Hyphenate all *in-laws*, and hyphenate all *great*-relatives:

Have you met my mother-in-law?

These three ladies are sisters-in-law.

This picture was taken with our great-great-grandfather.

*Grand*relatives are joined directly, without hyphens:

Our grandfather took the picture.

Colloquial descriptions. Informal speech has given rise to a number of colloquial descriptions that are hyphenated wherever they appear. Among these are:

He's a know-it-all and a stick-in-the-mud.

They have the know-how to get the job done.

Others include *Alice-sit-by-the-fire*, *Johnny-on-the-spot*, *light-o'-my-life*, and *stay-at-home*.

Compounds with letters. Use a hyphen when joining a capital letter to a word in instances such as these:

H-bomb	S-iron	U-boat	X-ray
I-beam	T-square	V-necked	

Ad hoc compounds. Writers sometimes form ad hoc compounds, compounds meant to serve an immediate and temporary purpose.

The remark was attributed to Richard Billings, a Las Vegas-lawyer-turned-desert developer.

He is an isolationist-traditionalist.

Such ad hoc compounds should be used sparingly, if ever, for they lump together too many thoughts for readers to handle easily.

6.3 Hyphens with Prefixes

Most prefixes are joined directly to their base words without the use of hyphens. Covered here are the typical uses in which hyphens are standard.

Prefixes to words beginning with capital letters.

A hyphen joins a prefix to a word that begins with a capital letter:

> No one was in the mood to attend the un-American rallies of the 1930s.

> Explorers unearthed numerous pre-Columbian artifacts.

In this same category are words such as *anti-Arab*, *pro-British*, *post-World War II*, *pre-McCarthy era*, and many others.

Prefixes of *all, ex, quasi,* or *self.*

When *all*, *ex*, *quasi*, or *self* is used as a prefix, a hyphen follows. This usage holds true whether the prefix and the base word form an adjective before a noun (section 6.4) or a compound word (section 6.2).

> The proposal called for an all-encompassing solution.

or Her proposed solution was all-encompassing.

> My ex-spouse has been hounding me to pay the money I owe her.

With regard to "ex-spouse" in the example just given, the prevalent style today is to substitute *former* without a hyphen:

> My former spouse has been hounding me . . .

> Former mayor (not *ex-mayor*) Garfield delivered the welcoming address.

Quasi is joined to its base word with a hyphen:

> By filing one document, the charity became a quasi-corporation.

> It was a quasi-academic argument.

The vast majority of *self* prefixes are hyphenated:

> Few little boys in a candy store could practice the self-restraint that he did.

> To rephrase the cliché, she is a self-made woman.

Exceptions: Dictionaries current at the writing of this book show *selfhood*, *selfless*, and *selfsame*, without hyphens. Other words beginning with *self* will probably come along and be formed without a hyphen.

Duplicated prefixes.
A hyphen is used to join duplicated prefixes:

> Let me re-redirect your attention to yesterday's testimony.

> The sub-subcommittee began its work yesterday.

Avoiding awkward or misleading prefixes.
Hyphens help to keep matters straight in sentences such as these:

> Congress favored a stiff anti-spy law (not "antispy").

> When her income tax refund came, she decided to re-cover the sofa (not "recover," as in "get back again").

> Measurements showed that the particles were un-ionized (not "unionized").

> Take time this weekend to re-create your special kinship with your family (not "recreate").

Similarly, hyphens are valuable in words such as *co-op* (not *coop*), *pre-position* (having to do with "before" and not *preposition*, referring to words), *re-sort* ("sort again"), and *re-treat* ("treat again").

6.4 Hyphens That Join Adjectives before a Noun

Use a hyphen between words, or between abbreviations and words, that form an adjective immediately before a noun. Use no hyphen if the adjective appears elsewhere in the sentence:

Live Aid raised money for starving people in drought-stricken areas.

but Large parts of Africa are drought stricken.

It is a large-scale project.

but The project is large scale.

You will have to get your staff involved in the decision-making process.

but He is a skilled decision maker.

The shale is purged by a fossil-fuel-fired steam generator.

but The shale is purged by a steam generator fired by fossil fuels.

The contractor tied in the roof-to-wall connection.

but The contractor tied in the connection from roof to wall.

Officials could do nothing about the situation on U.S.-owned property.

but Officials could do nothing about the situation on property that was owned by the U.S.

Testing was the subject of a U.S.-U.S.S.R. agreement.

but Testing was the subject of an agreement between the U.S. and the U.S.S.R.

"United 201, you are cleared for a straight-in approach."

but "Roger, tower. We will land straight in."

We are looking for five health-conscious, success-oriented people.

but We are looking for five people who are health conscious and success oriented.

He despised get-it-done, make-it-happen thinking.

but He despised thinking that said get it done, make it happen.

Long-lived and *short-lived*. *Long-lived* and *short-lived* are hyphenated wherever they appear:

It was a short-lived prophecy.

The prophecy was short-lived.

Well-known and similar compounds. Hyphens are used with adjectives that begin with *best, better, ill, lesser, little,* or *well.*

She is a well-known performer.

They formulated an ill-advised policy.

Exception: Hyphens are not used when the adjective follows the noun modified.

She is very well known.

The policy is ill advised.

Adjectives of color. Adjectives that describe color are hyphenated.

The iron-gray ship slowly sailed into view.

To save money they settled for black-and-white printing.

In some instances, adjectives that describe color are not hyphenated:

The floor was covered with black and white tiles.

Compound adjectives before a noun.

Compound adjectives— two or more words per adjective—
are hyphenated as shown here:

> The biggest establishment in town is the Circus-owned
> 600-room Edgewater Hotel.

> Water flowed today for the first time through the Folsom
> Lake-East Side diversion project.

> An old book dealt with the Herbert Hoover-Department of
> Agriculture program.

Some compound adjectives should be rewritten into a sentence. As an example, "He is a publisher-man of letters"
reads better as:

> He is a publisher and man of letters.

Similarly, "The transcontinental railroad was a product of
the Central Pacific-Union Pacific alliance" reads better as:

> The transcontinental railroad was the product of an alliance
> between the Central Pacific and the Union Pacific.

Cross-reference: This section has been about joining adjectives before a noun. For help with the opposite problem,
separating adjectives before a noun, see section 2.5.

6.5 Hyphens Not Necessary

Adverbs ending in *ly*.   Hyphens are not used
with adverbs that end in *ly*:

> It is a wholly owned subsidiary.

> The signal came from a rapidly approaching ship.

> For his age, he is an unusually well-preserved specimen.

When clarity isn't a problem. When an expression is easy to read and meaning is clear, hyphens are not necessary:

New Testament language is not as poetic as Old Testament language.

The wealthy live in Lake Shore Drive mansions.

County officials approved the child welfare plan.

Bids were taken on a new word processing system.

He attended speech correction class.

Her social security pension check came on the third of the month.

Because of the festivities, they took a longer than usual lunch period.

In the not too distant future we will be finished.

The company was licensed as a Class II carrier.

Roscoe's dairy produces grade A milk.

but The Roscoe family lived in an A-frame cabin (because "A-frame" is a compound word).

Foreign phrases. Do not use hyphens in phrases adapted from a foreign language:

He was convicted on prima facie evidence.

His statement was based on a priori analysis.

Phrases in quotation marks. Do not use a hyphen if a compound term is in quotation marks:

Our town adopted a "prior use" ordinance years ago.

6.6 The Suspensive Hyphen

When two or more words in a hyphenated compound have the same basic element and this element is mentioned in the last term only, a suspensive hyphen is used:

Old colleges are noted for their moss- and ivy-covered walls.

Before opening an account, he checked the long- and short-term interest rates.

They bought 8-, 10-, and 16-foot boards.

Gypsy Moth Egg-Mass Sampling with Fixed- and Variable-Radius Plots (Title of a U.S. Department of Agriculture booklet)

6.7 Hyphens with Titles

Double titles are hyphenated; single ones are not.

Double titles. Use a hyphen with double titles such as these:

He retired from his post as secretary-treasurer.

In an economy move, the organization created the post of treasurer-manager.

Pete Rose served as player-manager.

Single titles. Do not use a hyphen in titles such as these shown here:

William Henry Seward served as secretary of state.

Frederick Lord North was prime minister of England.

***Vice* as prefix.** Titles with *vice* in them may be written without hyphens:

Vice President Andrew Johnson followed Lincoln.

The vice commander was promoted last week.

It is correct, however, to hyphenate *vice-presidency*.

Suffixes to titles. A hyphen is used when *elect* or *designate* is suffixed to a title:

President-elect Wong called the meeting to order.

As ambassador-designate he was very careful with his remarks.

But use no hyphens if the name of the office is two or more words:

The vice president elect seemed to have kept on campaigning even though the elections were over.

6.8 Hyphens for Visual Effect

To avoid awkward-looking terms, hyphens should be used with words like *Inverness-shire*, *bell-like*, *gull-like*, and *hull-less*.

Although we have grown used to seeing *cooperate* and *coordinate* without a hyphen after *co*, *semi-independent* and *semi-indirect* are easier to follow with the hyphens, perhaps because the *ii* would be a visual burden.

Along these same lines, many readers will handle *nonnative* easier than *nonnative*, and *co-worker* will be more pleasing to the eye (and the mind) than *coworker*.

In short, many problems with the joining of words can be solved by adding a hyphen, not taking one out.

6.9 The Slant Bar (/) and the Joining of Words

The slant bar (/) has come into accepted usage in place of *per*, and mathematical shorthand frequently leads to expressions such as *feet/second* or *barrels/day*. The use of the slant bar in those constructions doesn't seem to pose any problem in meaning, even though many readers prefer to see things spelled out: *feet per second, barrels per day*.

In the writing of text, however, the meaning of the slant bar is far from definite. You might think the meaning to be definite if you were to check *Webster's Ninth New Collegiate Dictionary* under the word *diagonal*. There the meaning of the slant bar is given as ''or.''

A dictionary doesn't necessarily provide the final verdict, however, as can be demonstrated with the expression *and/or*. As the eminent scholar of legal language David Mellinkoff pointed out in his *Language of the Law*, the courts have assigned at least three meanings to *and/or*.

Therefore, all we know for certain is that the slant means at least ''or,'' and it could mean more.

So when considering the use of the slant bar, remember:

1. Don't use a slant bar in place of a hyphen. A hyphen joins the words in text or breaks them at the end of a line.
2. Don't use a slant bar in place of ''or.'' If you mean to say ''or,'' write it out. Write ''reading or writing skills,'' not ''reading/writing skills.''
3. Don't trust the slant bar to carry any particular meaning. If you mean to say ''horses, sheep, or both,'' then write it that way, not as ''horses and/or sheep.''

6.10 End-of-Line Breaks: A List of Don'ts

There was a time when writers didn't concern themselves with the breaking of a word at the end of a line. Manuscripts and school papers were, as they still should be, submitted with no end-of-line breaks, and the typesetter decided where end-of-line breaks would appear in the finished product.

Times change, in this case quite a bit. The increasing use of word processing systems makes it possible for an office or a cottage industry to turn out newsletters, pamphlets, brochures, and even bound books. These are finished products, often with words divided at the ends of lines, but seldom checked over by an editor or typesetter.

To make matters worse, some automated text-processing systems, or their operators, pay no heed to the most fundamental rules of end-of-line division. Consequently, we see one-syllable words such as *which* converted into two syllables at the end of a line: ''whi-ch.''

In addition, anyone who writes or types a letter or memo should be concerned about the correctness of end-of-line breaks.

Accordingly, the job description of being a writer includes knowing how to divide a word at the end of a line. What to do is quite simple: Keep a dictionary handy and use it.

A dictionary uses a raised dot to show where to break a word: *en·joy·ment, pres·ence, struc·tur·al*. When dividing the word in text, the hyphen goes at the end of a line, never the beginning.

With the help of a dictionary, you can decide on some of the more common divisions, such as these:

l endings—*con·verti·ble*, not *con·verti·ble*; *read·able*, not *reada·ble*

ing endings—*sail·ing*, not *sai·ling*; *in·trigu·ing*, not *in·trig·uing*; *re·vok·ing*, not *re·vo·king*

ab·hor·ring, not *ab·horr·ing*; *oc·cur·ring*, not *oc·curr·ing*

Although the vast majority of breaks can be handled by referring to a dictionary, not all of the syllable divisions in a dictionary are acceptable in prose.

Therefore, the list of don'ts given here is meant to supplement the advice in a dictionary.

1. Don't divide a one-syllable word.
2. Don't divide a one-syllable sound. Some words give the appearance of having more than one syllable but are pronounced as one-syllable sounds. Among these are words with *ed* endings, words such as *climbed*, *passed*, and *spelled*.

   Other one-syllable sounds that are not to be divided include these word endings:

cial	gion	tial
cion	gious	tion
cious	sial	tious

   As an example, *special* would be divided as *spe·cial*, never *spe·ci·al* or *speci·al*.
3. Don't make a one-letter division. That is, don't divide words such as these:

acre	even	over
around	idol	unite

4. Don't create awkward divisions. Here you will have to rely a lot on judgment and caution. Keep in mind that a person's name looks strange when spelled over two lines, and it's impossible to divide *assassin* without raising readers' eyebrows.
5. Don't divide abbreviations or the initials of a person's name. Spell out *NATO* on one line rather than divide *NA·TO*. Similarly, *T. S. Eliot* should be written on one line; if necessary, break it as *T. S.·Eliot*, but never *T.·S. Eliot*.

6. Don't divide large numbers expressed as figures. Readers will find it easier to understand *186,000 miles per hour* than *186,·000 miles per hour*.

7. Don't begin a line with a two-letter division. A two-letter division at the end of a line (*pa·tience*) is permissible, but a two-letter division should not be carried over to the next line if at all possible. As an example, write *wholly,* not *whol·ly*.

8. Don't rebreak a hyphenated compound. A hyphenated compound such as *forget-me-not* should be broken at the hyphens (*forget·me·not*) and not as *for·get·me·not*.

9. Don't divide prefixes. *Pseudo·scientific* is better than *pseu·doscientific*.

Try to avoid, if possible:

1. Dividing at the ends of more than two successive lines.

2. Dividing the last word of a paragraph; if you must divide it, carry over at least four letters to the next line.

3. Dividing the last word on a right-hand page.

4. Separating an identifier such as (a) or (1) from the matter to which it pertains.

Chapter 7. To Show Possession

You show possession in most instances by adding an apostrophe to a noun or by adding an apostrophe and an *s*. Often the choice is determined not by some rigid grammatical rule but by whether a word sounds right with one, two, or even three *s*'s tacked onto the end of it.

You can also show possession by using a personal pronoun such as *his* or *ours*.

And you have to keep straight the instances where an apostrophe is used in terms that aren't possessive.

And for still more on the apostrophe, see:

7.1 To Show Singular Possession

Singular noun not ending in *s*. The possessive form of a singular noun not ending in *s* is formed by adding an apostrophe and an *s*:

The ruckus started when he stepped on the dog's tail.

They ordered the chef's special.

It's the city's most comprehensive record shop.

Coke is made according to the company's secret formula.

Why is she wearing a man's hat?

Singular noun ending with an *s* or an *s* sound. Here advice on style varies. One school of thought says that the possessive form of a singular noun ending in *s* or an *s* sound should be formed by adding the apostrophe and the *s*. The other school says that you can get by with adding only the apostrophe.

According to the first school of thought, you would write "The proprietess's rules proved to be a bother." According to the second, you would write "The proprietess' rules proved to be a bother."

Because we tend to hear the sounds that language makes while we read, we will tend to hear the possessive *s*. Therefore, let's go all the way and add the *s*, in this case anyway; exceptions will be mentioned later.

Accordingly, this book recommends that you add the apostrophe and the *s* when forming the possessive of a singular noun ending in *s*. You would write:

Bette Davis's story proved to be a best-seller.

He liked the 300-ZX's paint job.

Additional examples are:

baroness's jewels
Berlioz's opera
Butz's policies
Charles's tonsils
cutlass's crew
fox's lair
governess's privilege
Levitz's Big Sale!
Mays's home run
Marx's theories
middle class's great hopes
witness's testimony

The rule just given should not be applied if it will lead to awkward-sounding constructions. For instance, it would appear to be correct to write "The lens's surface needs polishing." However, that sentence has an overweight *s* sound, and you would be better off if you wrote:

The surface of the lens needs polishing.

Tradition has left us with an apostrophe but no added *s* in these constructions:

in Jesus' name
Moses' laws

Both of the above would sound better if written as ''in the name of Jesus'' and ''the laws of Moses.''

7.2 To Show Plural Possession

Plural nouns not ending in *s*. Some plural nouns do not end in *s*. When writing with those nouns, add an apostrophe and an *s*:

The children's toys were scattered all over the floor.

Men's and women's shoes are on sale today.

They gratefully accepted the alumni's contributions.

Plural nouns ending in *s*. In many cases, a singular noun becomes plural by adding an *s*, thereby forming a plural noun. The plural noun then becomes a plural possessive by placing an apostrophe after the *s*:

They formed a patients' rights committee.

Management contended that the players' money demands were excessive.

Don't place a dollar value on our infants' lives.

Arguments over states' rights are old stuff.

They could not keep up with the Joneses' life-style.

7.3 Possessive Forms of Nouns Ending in an *eez* Sound

To avoid awkward-sounding endings, an apostrophe without the *s* is used to form the possessive of a word ending with an *eez* sound:

Hercules' labors are the subject of a great story.

Xerxes' troops put down revolts in Egypt and Babylonia.

The aborigines' traditions are going the way of the people.

7.4 Possessive Forms of Nouns the Same in Singular and Plural

When forming the possessive of a noun that is spelled the same whether singular or plural, add an apostrophe and an *s* to a noun not ending in *s* but an apostrophe only to a noun ending in *s*. This style applies whether singular or plural is meant:

The corps' location was treated as a secret.

As neophyte hunters, they quickly lost the three deer's tracks.

7.5 Possessive Forms of Nouns Plural in Form, Singular in Meaning

To show possession with a noun that is plural in form but singular in meaning, add the apostrophe only:

General Motors' profits were an item of discussion.

He wanted to emphasize mathematics' rigidity.

The sound of that last example can be improved by rewriting it to read:

He wanted to emphasize the rigidity of mathematics.

7.6 Double Possessives

A double possessive is an expression such as "I am a friend of Raoul's." In a double possessive, the word *of* is used in its possessive function, and some form of possessive noun is used. Another example is this one:

This is a cat of my nephew's.

Other forms of double possessives are these:

This wonderful land of ours.

Sonia is a friend of mine.

7.7 Possession by Inanimate Objects

Granted, an inanimate object such as a table doesn't own anything, but it's still acceptable to write:

The table's leg was broken.

The factory's whistle was silent.

Blueberry compote is tonight's dessert.

7.8 Possessive Forms of Compound Nouns

When using a compound noun, add an apostrophe and an *s* to the noun nearest the item possessed:

The attorney general's opinion became a matter of record.

That was an example of a singular possession by a compound noun. Keep in mind that if you were to convert *attorney general* (singular) to its plural form *attorneys general*, no *s* is added to the last noun. Thus the plural possessive is *not* formed by adding an *s* and an apostrophe, as with many other plural possessives. In this case, add an apostrophe and an *s*:

The attorneys general's opinions became a matter of record.

Similarly:

The brothers-in-law's books did not balance.

In instances such as these, you will probably like the looks of the expressions better if you rewrite them:

The opinions of the attorneys general became a matter of record.

Books kept by the brothers-in-law did not balance.

7.9 Alternative and Joint Possession

Alternative possession occurs when each noun individually possesses something. Joint possession occurs when the nouns together possess something.

Alternative possession. When constructing an alternative possession, show possession on each element:

These same problems arose during Nixon's and Reagan's administrations.

Mr. Gonzalez's and Mr. Koya's children made up half of the Little League team.

Joint possession. When constructing a joint possession, show possession on the last element of the series:

Jones and McCoughlin's department store had its annual sale early.

When Green and Bronowski's theory is applied, the results are different.

or   When the Green-Bronowski theory is applied, the results are different.

7.10 Apostrophe with Holidays, Names, and Titles

Holidays.   Use of the apostrophe with popular holidays is as shown here:

April Fools' Day	Mother's Day
Father's Day	New Year's Day

Names and titles.   Use of the apostrophe with names and titles varies. For instance, we have Hudson Bay but Hudson's Bay Company, Harpers Ferry but Martha's Vineyard, Columbia University Teachers College but Young Men's Christian Association, and *Publishers Weekly* but *Ladies' Home Journal*.

If in doubt, check with the originator of the term or consult a current reference work.

7.11 Apostrophes and Descriptive Terms

Apostrophes are seldom used with terms that are more descriptive than possessive:

Before you can receive a permit, you must take a test on citizens band radio rules.

They attended a House of Representatives session.

Similarly, when a person's name is used to identify a disease, syndrome, or something similar, the name is not made into a possessive:

He was afflicted with Down syndrome.

Other examples, from the *Stylebook/Editorial Manual* of the American Medical Association, are:

Ewing sarcoma   Parkinson disease
Hodgkin disease   Raynaud disease

7.12 Apostrophe with Traditional Expressions

For perhaps no reason other than tradition, an apostrophe without the *s* is used with *appearance' sake, conscience' sake, goodness' sake,* and *righteousness' sake*.

"For goodness' sake," she lamented, "what have you done now?"

If you were to write the expression without the word *sake*, the apostrophe-*s* combination would be correct:

My conscience's voice told me I had done wrong.

An apostrophe is used with popular expressions such as these:

I am at my wit's end.

Our house is but a stone's throw from where you live.

You get your money's worth at that restaurant.

7.13 Possessives and Italics

When writing an italicized term, the possessive ending should not be placed in italics:

Esquire's 50th anniversary issue was a big one.

The Publicity Handbook's suggestions on news releases should be followed.

Of course, a possessive in the title is italicized along with the rest of the title:

Barron's is a valuable source of information.

7.14 Possessive Pronouns

Use of the apostrophe.   Use an apostrophe when forming the possessive of pronouns such as shown here:

They relied on someone else's plans.

It is anyone's guess.

They borrowed each other's notes.

Others' plans have failed.

Apostrophe not used.   An apostrophe is not used when forming the possessive of *mine, our, ours, your, yours, his, hers, its, their, theirs,* or *whose*:

It is our house.

This house is ours.

The car is theirs.

Whose sweater is that?

Do not write *it's* ("it is") for the possessive *its*.

Do not write *there* ("place") or *they're* ("they are") for the possessive *their*.

Do not write *who's* ("who is") for the possessive *whose*.

Do not write *you're* ("you are") for the possessive *your*.

7.15 Possessives and Matters of Style

The item possessed need not follow directly after the name of the possessor. Both of the following are correct; which one you use depends upon your style of writing and how well your choice fits in with the sentence that comes before or that follows:

This is Ahmed's house.

This house is Ahmed's.

Awkward possessives should be rewritten even if more words are necessary. Don't write "the Department of Education's proposal" when this is better:

A proposal made by the Department of Education would . . .

Similarly, the use of the apostrophe in this sentence is correct, "They objected to the foreman's leaving early," even though the foreman doesn't possess "leaving early."

7.16 Plural, Not Possessive

When forming the plural of a word, use an *s* or an *es* on the end. No apostrophe is used:

We've had two cold Novembers in a row.

They tried to keep up with the Joneses.

The bar order consisted of three martinis and two gin fizzes.

He owned two Nissan 300-ZXes at one time.

Keep in mind that some words change spelling when going from singular to plural:

One company filed for bankruptcy last month, and two companies failed this month.

Chapter 8. Punctuation with Numbers

In addition to showing the uses of punctuation with numbers, this chapter deals with the related items of when to spell out numbers or write them as numerals, how to use abbreviations and symbols with numbers, and clarity in the writing of numbers.

8.1 General Principles for Using Numbers

Numerals or words—the general rule.

Whether to write numbers as numerals or spelled out as words has been the subject of two general rules for quite some time. One rule says to spell out whole numbers from one through nine. The other rule says to spell out whole numbers from one through ninety-nine. The first rule applies to writers in business, journalism, scientific or technical fields, and, increasingly, the humanities. The second rule applies primarily to writers producing fiction.

Regardless of subject and field, more and more editors, writers, and publishers are choosing numerals over spelled-out numbers. These reasons can be given: Readers grasp numerals more quickly than spelled-out numbers, and numerals are easier and faster to write than awkward, long combinations of spelled-out numbers. In addition, as we become more and more of a computer-oriented society, we will probably become more and more of a numeral-oriented society.

Still, writers of dialogue and fictional narratives will probably lean toward spelled-out numbers for a long time to come. After all, people don't talk in numerals; they talk in words, and it looks strange to see a character saying in print, "Last night I told you I loved you 10 times over."

What all of this means is that you must follow these steps when using this chapter:

1. Note the differences between the Rule of 9 and the Rule of 99 as shown below. The Rule of 9 applies to the vast majority of business, journalistic, and scientific subjects, and, increasingly, to the humanities. The Rule of 99 pertains mainly to fiction and some essays.

2. When a particular type of writing requires the use of spelled-out numbers, follow the styles shown under the Rule of 99.

Rule of 9	*Rule of 99*
man of 52	man of fifty-two
76th birthday	seventy-sixth birthday
50 million degrees Fahrenheit	fifty million degrees Fahrenheit
size 10 dress	size ten dress
$0.87 or 87 cents	eighty-seven cents
10th Amendment	Tenth Amendment
19th century	nineteenth century
Gay '90s	Gay Nineties
13×10^6 *or* 13 million	thirteen million

Cross-reference: For writing indefinite and round numbers, see section 8.18.

Cardinal numbers versus ordinal numbers.
A cardinal number is a number such as eight, 55, or 101. An ordinal number is a number such as eighth, 55th, or 101st.

When using numerals for the ordinal numbers second and third, write *2d* and *3d,* not *2nd* and *3rd* (no *n,* no *r*).

Matters of consistency.
Treat like subjects alike. That is, if you must use numerals for one of the

numbers pertaining to a subject, then use numerals for all references to that subject:

> For every five questionnaires mailed, three were returned, and the results will be announced in 6 to 18 months.

> A sample of 750 essays was selected from the top quarter and the bottom half for each of nine topics assigned; 683 essays were written on the first four topics, but only 67 on the last five.

In addition, this list of don'ts applies to the use of numbers.

Don't use numerals at the start of a sentence or a heading. Either write out the number or recast the sentence:

> Nineteen eighty-eight is a presidential election year.

> In 1988 the nation will elect a president.

Don't mix cardinal and ordinal numbers to mean the same thing. Do not write, ''Rankings were first, third, eight, and nine.'' Instead write:

> Rankings were first, third, eighth, and ninth.

Don't mix complete numbers with abbreviations of numbers. Instead of writing ''1920s and '30s,'' write:

> We need a popular history book of the 1920s and 1930s.

or We need a popular history book of the '20s and '30s.

or We need a popular history book of the twenties and thirties.

8.2 Abbreviations and Symbols with Numbers

When an abbreviation or a symbol is used with a number, the quantity is written as a numeral and not spelled out. Punctuation is as follows: (1) When the expression forms a compound adjective before a noun, a hyphen joins the terms in the adjective; (2) otherwise, a space is placed between a numeral and the abbreviation but not between the numeral and the symbol.

reading of 6.3 V	a 16-mm film
output of 45 MW	capacity of 24 sq. ft.
9′ × 11′	27° to 33°
8 cm	limit of 55 MPH
200 m^2	a 6-mg dose

Abbreviations of units of measure are the same in singular and plural:

Trap dimensions are 1 m by 13 m.

8.3 Addresses and Telephone Numbers

Punctuation of addresses varies and depends upon whether the address is written in a sentence or is block indented.

Addresses within a sentence.   Use commas to separate the parts of an address written in a sentence:

The resident ranger's office is in Ephrata, Washington.

For further information, write to Kelly O'Day, Resident Ranger, P. O. Box 630, Ephrata, WA 98823.

Addresses in block-indented style.

The address just given would appear as below in block-indented style:

Kelly O'Day, Resident Ranger
P. O. Box 630
Ephrata, WA 98823

No comma separates the state and the ZIP code. In addition, the decision whether to spell out the state name or use the U.S. Postal Service's two-letter abbreviation depends upon these factors:

1. Do not use the two-letter abbreviation in descriptive or narrative writing. As an example, it would be wrong to write, "Rioting broke out last night on a beach in Chicago, IL." Spell out *Illinois*.
2. Using the two-letter abbreviation with an address given in the text of a business letter is acceptable. Some writers don't like the looks of the abbreviation so they spell out the state name in full. Other writers prefer to use the abbreviation so that readers will have it handy to use with return correspondence. The choice is up to you or the organization you write for.
3. Use the two-letter abbreviation on the outside address of letters and packages. A list of two-letter abbreviations is at the end of this section.

To block indent an address in a letter, follow these instructions: Double-space above and below the block-indented address, assuming that the letter is single-spaced, which it should be. Type the address single-spaced, and indent it so that it is centered on the page.

Introductory punctuation with a block-indented address is usually a colon. Section 3.2, "Introductory Punctuation with Quotations," covers the principles involved.

Table of two-letter Postal Service abbreviations.

The U.S. Postal Service two-letter state abbreviations shown below are written in capital letters and left unpunctuated.

Included in the table are abbreviations for American Samoa, the District of Columbia, Guam, the Northern Mariana Islands, Puerto Rico, the Trust Territories, and the Virgin Islands.

State	Abbr.	State	Abbr.
Alabama	AL	Montana	MT
Alaska	AK	Nebraska	NE
American Samoa	AS	Nevada	NV
Arizona	AZ	New Hampshire	NH
Arkansas	AR	New Jersey	NJ
California	CA	New Mexico	NM
Colorado	CO	New York	NY
Connecticut	CT	North Carolina	NC
Delaware	DE	North Dakota	ND
Dist. of Columbia	DC	No. Mariana Is.	CM
Florida	FL	Ohio	OH
Georgia	GA	Oklahoma	OK
Guam	GU	Oregon	OR
Hawaii	HI	Pennsylvania	PA
Idaho	ID	Puerto Rico	PR
Illinois	IL	Rhode Island	RI
Indiana	IN	South Carolina	SC
Iowa	IA	South Dakota	SD
Kansas	KS	Tennessee	TN
Kentucky	KY	Texas	TX
Louisiana	LA	Trust Territories	TT
Maine	ME	Utah	UT
Maryland	MD	Vermont	VT
Massachusetts	MA	Virginia	VA
Michigan	MI	Virgin Islands	VI
Minnesota	MN	Washington	WA
Mississippi	MS	West Virginia	WV
Missouri	MO	Wisconsin	WI
		Wyoming	WY

Awkward-looking addresses.

An awkward-looking address can be avoided by using a mixture of numerals and spelled-out numbers. Instead of writing "666 5th Avenue," write:

Bantam Books is located at 666 Fifth Avenue.

You would carry the principle too far if you wrote "1021 One Hundred Twenty-first Street." In this case use all numerals, with a hyphen and spacing as shown:

Her address is at 1021 - 121st Street.

Room numbers.

Write room numbers in numerals and capitalize *room* when used with a number:

This class meets in West Hall, Room 111.

Telephone numbers.

Write telephone numbers in numerals and place parentheses around the area code. If an extension is given, abbreviate *extension*:

You may reach Ms. Takeda at (212) 435-0000, Ext. 611.

8.4 Ages

The style of writing ages follows these examples:

man of 52	age of 13
son six years old	seventh birthday
six-year-old son	76th birthday
25 years old	109th birthday

8.5 Binary Numbers

Binary numbers are written without commas or any other internal punctuation:

100001

8.6 Clarity and Combinations of Numbers

When several numbers appear before a noun, confusing appearances can be avoided by using words for some and numerals for others.

The order is for three 12-foot ladders.
Begin by ripping two ¾-inch boards.

Sometimes the solution is to rewrite the sentence. Either of the following is acceptable, but the second version's consistent use of numerals makes it easier to grasp:

In the first group of twelve hundred, 300 were symptom-free.

or In the first group, 300 of the 1,200 patients were symptom-free.

In any event, quick comprehension is not gained by writing: "In the first group of 1,200, 300 were symptom-free."

8.7 Clock Time

Clock time expressed as numerals.

Clock time is usually expressed as numerals, especially when the exact minute is important. A colon with no space on either side of it separates the hour from the minutes. The abbreviations *a.m.* and *p.m.* may be lowercased or capitalized and are punctuated with periods but no internal space:

Flight 647's departure time is 3:19 p.m.

Today's staff meeting begins promptly at 9:30 a.m.

All participants completed testing in 2 hr. 27 min.

No punctuation is used when referring to the 24-hour clock, and *a.m.* and *p.m.* are not used either:

Flight 647's departure time is 1519.

Today's staff meeting begins promptly at 0930.

Time written as words.
In narrative or in dialogue, words and not numerals are usually used for even, half, and quarter hours:

The director said that the staff meeting begins at half past nine.

"Dinner will be served at seven," the hostess announced.

The bridge is closed from midnight until noon.

8.8 Compound Numerical Adjectives before a Noun

When using a number to form a compound adjective before a noun, join the parts of the adjective with a hyphen:

Employees liked the four-day work week.

Congress approved a five-cent-per-bottle tax.

The captain announced a 10-minute delay.

8.9 Dates

No punctuation is necessary when a date is written only as a month and year:

Someone will be appointed to arrange the May 1987 convention.

When a day of the month is added, a comma separates the day from the year:

The society's next convention will convene on May 21, 1987.

When a complete date—month, day, and year—is written into a sentence, the question arises whether to place a comma after the year. Either style shown in the next two examples is acceptable, as long as the same style is followed throughout:

The May 21, 1987, convention has been rescheduled.
The May 21, 1987 convention has been rescheduled.

Four different styles of writing dates are now in use. The styles, and comments about them, are:

May 21, 1987—Order is month, day, year. A comma and a space separate the day from the year. The traditional method of showing a date.

21 May 1987—Order is day, month, year. Internal punctuation is not used. This style of writing dates is used in the military and in some scholarly and scientific publications.

1987-05-21—Order is year, month, day. Hyphens are used between year and month and between month and day. Used in some computer applications and always with 10 keystrokes. Months and days of less than two digits

will have to have a zero placed in front of
them to make 10 keystrokes, as in 1987-
01-01 (January 1, 1987).

5/21/87—Order is month, day, year. Slant bars are
used to separate internal elements. Use is
limited to informal correspondence.

8.10 Decimals

Use a zero to the left of the decimal point if no value
applies. Use a zero to the right of the decimal point only to
show exact measurement:

measured height of 16.0 feet	1.35 inches
but .50-caliber bullet	0.35 inches

In some scientific publications, spaces separate three-digit
segments to the right of the decimal point. Accordingly, pi is
written as 3.14159 or 3.141 59.

8.11 Degrees of Measurement

Punctuation with degrees of measurement is as shown below:

36°30′N (no space between degrees, minutes, and symbols)

20° C (no period after C) *or* 20 degrees Celsius

an angle of 16° *or* an angle of 16 degrees

50 million degrees Fahrenheit

8.12 Dimensions and Sizes

When writing dimensions and sizes, the usual practice is to
write numbers as numerals while spelling out units of
measurement:

6 feet 2 inches tall
6-foot-2-inch man
7 meters wide by 18 meters long
4 × 4 matrix
size 10 dress
size 38 regular
8½-by-11-inch paper
3-by-5 cards *or*, more precisely,
    3-inch-by-5-inch cards *or* 3"- × -5" cards

8.13 Distances and Speeds

When writing distances or speeds, use a hyphen if the value is a compound adjective:

journey of 10 miles
a five-mile trip
the 12-mile limit
velocity of 1,600 feet per second
a 15-knot wind
speed of eight miles per hour

8.14 Formal Documents and Numbers

In formal documents such as proclamations, numbers are spelled out:

In the year nineteen hundred and forty-one we set upon a dangerous mission.

The Eighty-second Congress now stands adjourned.

That nation's fiscal policies demonstrated the aptness of the cliché millions for defense but not one cent for tribute.

Be it hereby proclaimed that on this Fourth of July we are gathered to . . .

8.15 Fractions

Use a hyphen to form spelled-out fractions as shown below. Also use a hyphen when you prefix a fraction to a word or form a compound word of a fraction.

In addition, spell out a fraction when it is followed by *of a* or *of an*:

a ½-inch pipe	one-half of an inch
as many as 3¼ times	two two-hundredths
cut in one-half	twenty-five one-thousandths

8.16 Frequencies

When a frequency consists of four or more digits, use a comma between the third and fourth digit counting from the right:

$$20,000 \text{ hertz}$$

Exception: 1610 kilocycles

8.17 Inclusive Numbers

Inclusive numbers may be written with a hyphen:

Repeated testing yielded measurements of 6-9 volts.

The Russo-Finnish War was fought during the winter of 1939-1940.

To write "the winter of 1939-1940" is to write a statement of reasonably known values; this use of inclusive numbers poses no problems of clarity.

On the other hand, "6-9 volts" can mean "from 6 *to* 9 volts" or "from 6 *through* 9 volts." The first meaning may or may not include 9 volts; the second one definitely does.

Therefore, the presentation of inclusive numbers can be made more accurate by not using the hyphen and instead writing out what is meant. As an example:

Repeated testing yielded measurements of 6 through 9 volts.

8.18 Indefinite and Round Numbers

Indefinite and round numbers are usually spelled out:

As I said before, "A thousand times no!"

Thanks a million.

They say that upward of fifty thousand people were at the concert.

In a good year he sells between four and five hundred head of cattle.

Exceptions: Some cases call for numerals plus the words *million* or *billion*:

The population of the United States is 230 million.

Our planet earth is at least 4.5 billion years old.

8.19 Large Numbers

Large numbers are best written as numerals. Commas or spaces separate three-digit segments written to the left of the decimal point:

16,475 *or* 16 475
1,212 *or* 1 212
15,062.73 *or* 15 062.73
13×10^6 (*not* 13,000,000)

Exceptions:

binary numbers: 0010110
page numbers: page 1233
serial numers: 346177715

8.20 Metric (SI) Units

What we commonly call the metric system is more properly known as the *Système international d'unités*, abbreviated SI. It is a system in general use by scientists around the world.

Tables 8-1 through 8-3 show examples of SI units of measurements and conversions to SI units along with a list of numerical prefixes. The tables show the correct use of abbreviations, spacing, symbols, and terms.

Table 8-1
Examples of SI Units of Measurement

Quantity	Name	Symbol
	SI Unit	
acceleration	meter per second squared	m/s^2
activity (radioactive)	1 per second	s^{-1}
area	square meter	m^2
concentration (of amount of substance)	mole per cubic meter	mol/m^3
current density	ampere per square meter	A/m^2
density	kilogram per cubic meter	kg/m^3
luminance	candela per square meter	cd/m^2
magnetic field strength	ampere per meter	A/m
specific volume	cubic meter per kilogram	m^3/kg
speed, velocity	meter per second	m/s
volume	cubic meter	m^3
wave number	1 per meter	m^{-1}

Table 8-2
Numerical Prefixes in SI Measurement

Factor	Prefix	Symbol	Factor	Prefix	Symbol
10^{18}	exa	E	10^{-1}	deci	d
10^{15}	peta	P	10^{-2}	centi	c
10^{12}	tera	T	10^{-3}	milli	m
10^9	giga	G	10^{-6}	micro	μ
10^6	mega	M	10^{-9}	nano	n
10^3	kilo	k	10^{-12}	pico	p
10^2	hecto	h	10^{-15}	femto	f
10^1	deka	da	10^{-18}	atto	a

Table 8-3
Examples of Conversions to SI Units

Physical quantity	Traditional U.S. unit	SI equivalent
area	acre	4 046.873 m^2
	square foot*	0.092 903 04 m^2
	square inch*	645.16 mm^2
	square mile (statute)	2.589 998 km^2
	square yard	0.836 127 4 m^2
energy	British thermal unit	1 055. 056 J
	erg	10^{-7} J
	kilowatt hour*	3.6 × 10^6 J
force	dyne	10^{-5} N
	kilogram force*	9.806 65 N
length	foot (international)*	0.304 5 m
	inch*	2.54 cm
	mile (U.S. statute)	1.609 347 km
	nautical mile (international; nmi)*	1 852.0 m
	yard	0.914 4 m
mass	grain*	64.798 91 mg
	ounce	28.349 52 g
	pound (U.S.)*	0.453 592 37 kg
power	horsepower (electric)*	0.746 kW
pressure	atmosphere (normal)*	101 325.0 Pa
	pound per square inch (psi)	6 894.757 N/m^2
volume	cubic foot	0.028 316 85 m^3
	cubic inch	16.387 06 cm^3
	fluid ounce	29.573 53 mL
	quart (liquid)	0.946 352 9 L

* Conversion factors for these units are exact.
For conversion factors that are not exact, the precision with which the
quantity was measured determines the number of decimal places.

8.21 Money

Punctuation with money is as shown in the examples below. Cents are carried to two decimal places when there is a need to be specific. In addition, when you spell out the number, also spell out the unit of currency:

$3.25	$4.00 worth of candy
$0.87 or 87 cents	$410 net loss
five dollars	$300,000

Amounts of money of a million dollars or more are partly spelled out. The reason is to avoid excessive strings of zeros. Note that the dollar sign comes before the numeral and not where the word *dollars* would fall:

Investments totaled $11 million for the year, and sales amounted to $6 million.

The company's net worth is $1.25 billion.

8.22 Percentages

Use numerals to write percentages. The word *percent* is preferred in text. The percent symbol is preferred in tables and equations.

A space goes between the numeral and *percent;* no space is placed between the numeral and the symbol:

11 percent; 11%
0.5 percent; 0.5%
3 percentage points
range of 50 percent to 70 percent; 50% to 70%

8.23 Plurals of Numbers

Plurals of numerals. To form the plural of a numeral, add *s* alone:

He is a man in his 40s.

She participated in the revolutions of the 1930s.

Plurals of numbers spelled out. The plurals of spelled-out numbers are written like the plurals of other nouns:

They came in twos and threes.

He is a man in his forties.

We were all sixes and sevens.

8.24 Proportions and Ratios

Proportions. Proportions are expressed as numerals and written out:

Use 1 cup of flour to ½ cup of milk.

Ratios. Ratios are expressed as numerals and punctuated with a colon. No space is used on either side of the colon:

gear ratio of 3.73:1
calculated ratio of 1:53,000

8.25 Scores, Betting Odds, and Handicaps

Sports items such as scores, betting odds, and handicaps are written as numerals joined by a hyphen. The word *to* is seldom necessary, but when it is used it should be hyphenated:

The final score was 6-2 in favor of the Giants.

or The final score was 6-to-2 in favor of the Giants.

or The final score was Giants 6, Cubs 2.

Odds of 5-4 were posted at the start.

She plays with a 3-stroke handicap.

8.26 Serial Numbers

The popular concept of a serial number is that it is something like the identification number found on a car or television set or camera. Such a serial number might read "IB5100-6171."

In a stricter sense, a serial number is a number in a series of items produced. The items might be books, the parts of a book, or amendments to the Constitution.

Representative serial numbers are shown below. The punctuation of the original is retained. Numerals are preferred except for more formal uses:

First Amendment	page 6
10th Amendment	subsection II.1
Sociology 10-A	treatment protocol 10
chapter 2	*Document 95* (title of a publication)

8.27 Spelled-Out Numbers: How to Write

The simplest form of a spelled-out number is a single word such as *ten*, *fifty*, or *ninety*. When you start combining numbers into compound words, follow these rules.

Use a hyphen to connect a word ending in *y* to another word:

A twenty-first birthday is a big event.

She turned twenty-one today.

Do not use a hyphen, or any other punctuation, between other separate words that are part of one number:

Our company celebrated its one hundred twenty-first birthday this year.

This year our company celebrated birthday number one hundred twenty-one.

When you add it all up, it comes to one thousand one hundred fifty-five.

8.28 Suffixes with Numbers

***Odd* as a suffix.**   When you add *odd* as a suffix to a number, use a hyphen whether the term is spelled out or written with numerals:

The manuscript consisted of 420-odd pages.

Critics raved about the play, which ran for sixteen-hundred-odd performances.

He spoke for fifty-odd minutes.

A reader with a probing sense of humor will snicker at expressions like ''odd pages,'' ''odd performances,'' and "odd minutes," even though they're properly punctuated. Therefore, it might be better to use *approximately* or *about* and write "about 420 pages," "about sixteen hundred performances," or "approximately fifty minutes."

Suffixes of *fold, some, score,* or *square*.

When you suffix *fold, some, score,* or *square* to a number, follow these rules for use of the hyphen: (1) Use a hyphen if the compound is formed with a numeral and a word, but (2) do not use a hyphen if the compound is spelled out; instead write the term as a close compound:

Production increased 20-fold over a two-year period.

I stand foursquare behind you.

"They're quite a twosome, aren't they?"

8.29 Time Span and the Apostrophe

The apostrophe is used with time span in constructions like these:

Some people expect two weeks' pay for one day's work.

This plaque is presented in honor of Santiago Perreira's twenty-five years' service to the company.

Cross-reference: In this instance, the rules that apply are the same ones that govern the use of the apostrophe in singular and plural possession. See chapter 7.

8.30 Years and Longer Periods of Time

Numerals for years.   Years are best expressed as numerals. When the abbreviations B.C. or A.D. are used, they are capitalized. A space is placed between the year and the abbreviation. The abbreviations themselves are punctuated with periods but no spaces. Note that B.C. follows the year; A.D. comes before:

Our best year was 1976.

Gaius Caesar, a grandson of Augustus, was born in 20 B.C. and died in A.D. 4.

However, A.D. may appear after the time period in this type of construction:

Disease struck the village in the second century A.D.

Abbreviations of years.

Use an apostrophe to form the shorter form of a year:

The class of '80 held its five-year reunion late.

Paine exemplified the spirit of '76.

Prefixes with years.

Use a hyphen to join a prefix to a year:

Her novel was definitely a pre-1950 epic.

Combining successive years.

Successive years should be combined with a hyphen, not a slant bar:

Congress was late in acting on the budget for the 1980-81 fiscal year.

Several blizzards struck during the winter of 1978-79.

Decades and centuries.

When writing decades and centuries, use numerals in constructions like these:

Events of the 19th century seemed bound to repeat themselves.

Even though his feet were firmly planted in the 1970s, he was a serious student of the Gay '90s.

Spell out numbers in constructions such as these:

Nothing happened on the continent for four centuries.

He devoted the last three decades of his life to the project.

8.31 Zero

Spell out zero in constructions where no other numeral is used:

One pertinent topic today is zero-based budgeting.

When zero is written as a numeral, it should have a unit of measurement shown with it:

Values fell in the range from 0% to 6%.

Chapter 9. Punctuation with Documentation

Documentation shows readers where you obtained your material. In addition, documentation offers readers a list of references should they want to pursue the subject further.

The material presented in this chapter covers six types of documentation: bibliographies, name-and-page-number systems, name-and-year systems, numbered text references, notes with superior numbers, and notes with page numbers.

A seventh system is dealt with in section 3.15, ''Parenthetical References and Quotations.''

These various systems are used by writers in all fields, and no particular field in the sciences, humanities, or the popular press has a monopoly on any one style of documentation.

As used in this chapter, the word *article* means any article, essay, or short story in a periodical or chapter in a book—the smaller part of a larger publication. The word *book* refers to a book, proposal, report, booklet, pamphlet, or brochure—any complete publication.

9.1 Obtaining the Facts of Publication

The facts of publication constitute the items needed to write documentation. These items vary, depending upon whether the document is an article or a book.

Book. To obtain the facts of publication for a book, check the title page and the back of the title page. With some publications, such as documents produced by governmental or private organizations, some of the facts of publication are also found on the last pages of the work.

For a book, the facts of publication are:

Name or names of the author(s), editor(s), compiler(s), translator(s), or institution responsible for preparing the book.

Full title, including subtitle, if any.

Title of series, if any; number of books in series, if applicable; volume number, if any; edition number, if any.

Place of publication. Place of publication includes, as a minimum, the name of a city and frequently the name of a state, province, or country.

Name of publisher.

Date of publication. The date of publication is found on the *back* of the title page and is the latest copyright date. Do not use the latest printing date. The date you want is introduced with "Copyright" or the symbol ©.

Page numbers. For a bibliography entry, you do not need to copy the number of pages in the book. For notes or in-text references, you will need specific citations to a page or pages in the book.

Article.   Some of the facts of publication for an article are found on the first page of the article. Other facts of publication are found in front, near the table of contents. There you will find the complete name of the publication along with volume number, issue number, and date of publication.

For an article, the facts of publication are:

Name(s) of the author(s).

Title of the article.

Name of the periodical.

Volume number, if used; issue number, if used.

Date of publication.

Page numbers. For a bibliography, use inclusive pages occupied by the article. For notes or in-text references, use specific citations to a page or pages in the article.

9.2 Using the Facts of Publication

You are allowed to make minor changes to the facts of publication so that they will conform to the style of documentation.

Name of author.
Here *author* refers to the individual or organization responsible for writing, editing, compiling, translating, or otherwise preparing the publication.

If more than one name is listed as author, copy the names in sequence, even if the sequence is not in alphabetical order.

Drop any abbreviations of titles such as "M.D" or "Ph.D."

Titles.
The style of showing titles is given in sections 5.1 through 5.13. To summarize the material presented there, underline (italicize) titles of whole works such as books and reports, and place quotation marks around the titles of parts of works, which include articles and chapters of a book.

In documentation in the sciences, a different style of showing article titles is often used. In that style, quotation marks are omitted, and only the first letter of the title and any proper nouns are uppercased:

Johnson, D. J. A black-box mode of communication. *Computational Psychology*. 8:2 (February 1980), 31.

That style differs from the style taught in this book:

Johnson, D. J. "A Black-Box Mode of Communication." *Computational Psychology*. 8:2 (February 1980), 31.

Although the style taught here is the second one—the use of quotation marks and uppercased letters—writers should find it relatively easy to incorporate either style into documentation.

Numerals.
Numerals sometimes appear in titles and with any numbers used to identify volume, series, issue, or edition. If a Roman numeral appears in the title, leave the numeral in Roman. If a Roman numeral appears with volume, series, issue, or edition, change the numeral to Arabic.

Preface page numbers in Roman numerals are to be left in Roman.

Punctuation.
You may make minor changes to punctuation to adapt the facts of publication to your style of punctuation—provided that your changes do not alter the original meaning.

Such changes are rarely necessary, if authors are willing to temporarily accept someone else's style of punctuation.

Place of publication.

When showing the place of publication, the following cities can usually stand alone, that is, without any accompanying state, province, or country.

Amsterdam	Helsinki	Omaha
Atlanta	Hiroshima	Oslo
Baltimore	Honolulu	Ottawa
Belfast	Houston	Paris
Berlin	Indianapolis	Peking (Beijing)
Boston	Iowa City	Philadelphia
Brussels	Jerusalem	Pittsburgh
Budapest	Las Vegas	Prague
Buenos Aires	Leningrad	Quebec
Buffalo	Lisbon	Rio de Janeiro
Cairo	London	St. Louis
Calcutta	Los Angeles	St. Paul
Chicago	Louisville	Salt Lake City
Cincinnati	Madrid	San Diego
Cleveland	Melbourne	San Francisco
Copenhagen	Memphis	Seattle
Dallas	Mexico City	Shanghai
Denver	Miami	Singapore
Detroit	Milwaukee	Stockholm
Dublin	Minneapolis	Tokyo
Edinburgh	Montreal	Toronto
Geneva	Moscow	Vienna
Guatemala City	Naples	Warsaw
The Hague	New Delhi	
Havana	New Orleans	
	New York	
	Oklahoma City	

But: London, Ontario; Moscow, Idaho; Naples, Florida; Rome, New York; Vienna, Virginia. (Source: American Medical Association *Stylebook/Editorial Manual*)

Standard state abbreviations for use with place of publication are shown in this list:

State	*Abbreviation*
Alabama	Ala.
Alaska	Alaska
Arizona	Ariz.
Arkansas	Ark.
California	Calif.
Canal Zone	Canal Zone
Colorado	Colo.
Connecticut	Conn.
Delaware	Del.
District of Columbia	D.C.
Florida	Fla.
Georgia	Ga.
Guam	Guam
Hawaii	Hawaii
Idaho	Idaho
Illinois	Ill.
Indiana	Ind.
Iowa	Iowa
Kansas	Kan.
Kentucky	Ky.
Louisiana	La.
Maine	Me.
Maryland	Md.
Massachusetts	Mass.
Michigan	Mich.
Minnesota	Minn.
Mississippi	Miss.
Missouri	Mo.
Montana	Mont.
Nebraska	Neb.
Nevada	Nev.
New Hampshire	N.H.
New Jersey	N.J.
New Mexico	N.M.
New York	N.Y.
North Carolina	N.C.
North Dakota	N.D.
Ohio	Ohio

State	*Abbreviation*
Oklahoma	Okla.
Oregon	Ore.
Pennsylvania	Pa.
Puerto Rico	Puerto Rico
Rhode Island	R.I.
South Carolina	S.C.
South Dakota	S.D.
Tennessee	Tenn.
Texas	Tex.
Utah	Utah
Vermont	Vt.
Virginia	Va.
Washington	Wash.
West Virginia	W. Va.
Wisconsin	Wis.
Wyoming	Wyo.

U.S. Postal Service ZIP codes may also be used. See section 8.3.

Abbreviations for the parts of a document.

Acceptable abbreviations for the parts of a document are:

Part	*Abbreviation*
chapter	chap.
edition	ed.
Revised edition	Rev. ed.
Second edition	2d ed.
editor or editors	ed. or eds.
compiler or compilers	comp. or comps.
translator or translators	trans. (singular or plural)
page or pages	p. or pp.
Volume 4	Vol. 4
four volumes	4 vols.
Number 3	No. 3
Part 2	Pt. 2

Documentation can often be written without using the abbreviations ''Vol.,'' ''No.,'' and ''p.'' or ''pp.''

Use of page numbers. For a bibliography entry for a book, no need exists to copy the number of pages in the book. For a bibliography entry for an article, copy the inclusive pages of the article. When writing notes or other in-text references, you will have to copy specific page numbers.

When showing inclusive page numbers, use a hyphen between the page numbers and show all the numbers: 76-79, not 76-9; 101-105, not 101-5.

Missing facts of publication. When it is not possible to obtain all the facts of publication, abbreviations can be used:

Item	*Abbreviation*
place of publication not given	n.p.
publisher not given	n.p.
date of publication not given	n.d.
page number(s) not given	n. pag.

In documentation, the abbreviation is inserted where the missing fact of publication should go.

9.3 Bibliographies

A bibliography (or reference list) is a list of works consulted; it is placed after the text.

Items are arranged alphabetically, disregarding the articles *a, an,* and *the.* A long bibliography may be broken into sections for different chapters or sections based on topics or type of publications consulted. Within each section, items are listed alphabetically.

In a bibliography, authors' names are reversed, that is, given last name first. Periods separate the major elements of author, title, and publication data. Page numbers are not included for a book but are included for an article.

Book by one author. A bibliography entry for a book by a single author resembles this example:

Brinkley, Allan. *Voices of Protest: Huey Long, Father Coughlin, and the Great Depression*. New York: Alfred A. Knopf, 1982.

Book by two authors.

For two authors, commas are used to separate names:

Fadiman, Clifton, and Howard, James. *Empty Pages: A Search for Writing Competency in School and Society*. Belmont, Calif.: Fearon Pitman Publishers, Inc., 1979.

Book by three or more authors.

For three or more authors, semicolons are used to separate names:

Hanks, Kurt; Belliston, Larry; and Edwards, Dave. *Design Yourself!* Los Altos, Calif.: William Kaufmann, Inc., 1978.

When there are more than three authors, you could include the names of all the authors, space permitting. What is more commonly done is to use just the first author's name and the expression "and others" or "et al." If you use "et al." it is not underlined (italicized), and a period comes after "al." but not after "et."

Bradock, Richard, and others. *Research in Written Composition*. Urbana, Ill.: National Council of Teachers of English, 1963.

Book by authors with the same last names.

When authors have the same last names, repeat the names:

Christensen, Francis, and Christensen, Bonniejean. *Notes Toward a New Rhetoric: Nine Essays for Teachers*. 2d ed. New York: Harper & Row Publishers, Inc., 1978.

Book by an organization.

When an organization is the writer of a document, the bibliographic style is the same as for a document by a single author:

National Archives and Records Service. *Plain Letters*. Washington, D.C.: U.S. Government Printing Office, 1973.

Book by an author with a pen name.
Use the pen name of an author when that is what the title page shows. No need exists to supply the real name, for library catalogs provide plenty of cross-references. Punctuation follows the style for a book by one author.

Book with author's name not given.
If the author's name is known but not given on the title page, the bibliography entry shows the name in brackets. Note that the period goes inside the brackets:

[Harrington, Charles.] *The Deacon's Surprise, and Other Follies*. London, 1733.

If the name of the author involves guesswork, a question mark is placed inside the brackets:

[Harrington, Charles?] *The Deacon's Surprise, and Other Follies*. London, 1733.

If the author's name (or the name of the editor, compiler, or translator) is neither given nor ascertainable, begin the bibliography entry with the title of the work. Do not use ''anon.'' or ''anonymous.''

Air Pollution Primer. New York: National Tuberculosis and Respiratory Disease Association, 1971.

Book with author's name supplied.
If the title page shows an author's last name plus initials and if you know the author's full name, you could supply the name as a convenience to readers. The technique involves the use of brackets:

Hayakawa, S[amuel] I[chiye]. *Language in Thought and Action*. 4th ed. New York: Harcourt Brace Jovanovich, 1978.

Book with editor, compiler, or translator in place of author.

A bibliography item begins with the name of a book's editor, compiler, or translator when one of these is listed on the title page and no author's name is given. "Editor" or other term is abbreviated and placed after the name:

Lawlor, Joseph, ed. *Computers in Composition Instruction*. Los Alamitos, Calif.: SWRL Educational Research and Development, 1982.

Mandelbaum, Allen, trans. *The Aeneid of Virgil*. New York: Bantam Books, 1971.

Cooper, Charles R., and Odell, Lee, eds. *Research on Composing: Points of Departure*. Urbana, Ill.: National Council of Teachers of English, 1978.

Book with editor, compiler, or translator in addition to author.

When an author's name appears on the title page along with the name of an editor, compiler, or translator, begin the bibliography entry with the author's name. Place the name of the editor, compiler, or translator after the title:

Twain, Mark. *Adventures of Huckleberry Finn*. Edited by Henry Nash Smith. Boston: Houghton Mifflin Co., 1958.

Book edition, series, or volume.

The edition, series, or volume is placed after the title of a book:

Himstreet, William C., and Baty, Wayne Murlin. *Business Communications: Principles and Methods*. 7th ed. Boston: Kent Publishing Company, 1984.

Mencken, H. L. *The American Language: An Inquiry into the Development of English in the United States*. 4th ed., corrected, enlarged, and rewritten. New York: Alfred A. Knopf, 1936.

Mencken, H. L. *The American Language: An Inquiry into the Development of English in the United States*. Supplement 1. New York: Alfred A. Knopf, 1945.

Handbook on California's Natural Resources. Vol. 2. Sacramento, Calif.: Resources Agency of California, 1970.

Churchill, Winston E. *The Second World War*. 6 vols. Boston: Houghton Mifflin Co., 1948.

Tierney, Brian, and others, eds. *The Origins of Modern Imperialism—Ideological or Economic?* Random House Historical Issues Series, No. 19. New York: Random House, Inc., 1967.

Book in a reprinted edition. When writing an entry for a reprinted edition of a book, data on the reprinting publisher is given after data on the original publisher:

Bierce, Ambrose. *The Devil's Dictionary.* Neale Publishing Co., 1911. Reprint. New York: Dover Publications, Inc., 1958.

Unpublished work. An unpublished work such as a thesis, manuscript, or book in draft is treated the same as a published book but with two exceptions. The title is placed in quotation marks and not italics, and the word *thesis* or similar is used to label the work:

Willoughby, Thomas H. "Student Evaluation of California State Service." M.A. thesis. Sacramento, Cal.: California State University, Sacramento, 1959.

Articles. The instructions for listing articles in a bibliography pertain to articles, essays, or stories in a periodical.

When listing articles, list authors' names in the same manner that you would list authors' names for books. Then give title of the article in quotation marks, title of the periodical underlined (italicized), volume number and issue number and date, and the inclusive pages that the article appeared on.

The abbreviations "Vol.," "No.," and "p." or "pp." will not be necessary if these references are handled as shown here:

• When you know only the volume number, simply show it as an Arabic number—16.

- When you know volume and issue number, separate the two with a colon—16:4.
- When adding page numbers, set them off with a comma—16:4, 27-31.
- In practice, the date of publication is placed in parentheses after the volume and issue—16:4 (April 1979), 27-31.

Arnold, Lois V. "Writer's Cramp and Eyestrain—Are They Paying Off?" *English Journal.* 53 (January 1964), 10-15.

"Word Processing: How Will It Shape the Student as a Writer?" *Classroom Computer News* (November/ December 1982), 24-27, 74-76.

Martin, F.; Roberts, K.; and Collins, A. "Short-term Memory for Sentences." *Journal of Verbal Learning and Verbal Behavior.* 7 (1968), 560-566.

Pindera, J. T., and Sze, Y. "Creep of Some Gasket Materials." *Transactions of the Canadian Society of Mechanical Engineers.* 1:2 (June 1972), 101-105.

Hasan, M. A., and others. "Energy Losses of Positive and Negative High-Energy Channeled Particles." *Physical Review A.* 27:1 (January 1983), 395-407.

Hunter, Bill. "Foggy Financial Reports." *Industry Week* (April 5, 1982), 37-39.

"Compact-Disc Players." *Consumer Reports.* 50:6 (June 1985), 324-329.

With newspapers, it is sometimes necessary to give the section number or name with the page number:

Clines, Francis X. "The Mother Tongue Has a Movement." *New York Times* (June 3, 1984), 8E.

Corwin, Miles. "A City with Its Own 'Official Language.' " *San Francisco Chronicle* (May 19, 1985), *Punch,* 3.

When an article is "continued," give the page that the article starts on and the page or pages on which it continues. A comma separates the pages:

"Government, Business Try Plain English for a Change."
U.S. News & World Report (Nov. 7, 1977), 46, 51.

Work cited in another work.   On occasion you will want to refer to a work cited in another work, such as an article mentioned in another article or book. Because readers might want to try to find either work, you should give as much information as you can about both. An example is this one:

> Walpole, Jane R. "Why Must the Passive Be Damned?"
> *College Composition and Communication*. 30:3 (October 1979), 251. In Bush, Don. "The Passive Voice Should Be Avoided—Sometimes." *Technical Communication*. 28:1 (First Quarter 1981), 19-20, 22.

This same technique can be used to refer to a chapter in a book. The example below mentions a chapter in a book by the same author.

> Ringer, Robert J. "How People Get the Things They Want." Chapter 3 in *Restoring the American Dream*. New York: Fawcett Crest Books, 1979, 71-120.

Government documents.   When a government document is produced by an agency, follow the style shown for a book by an organization. If the author(s) name or names are known, use the style appropriate to the number of names.

Computer software.   When writing a bibliography entry for a computer software program, include the writer of the program, if known; the title of the program underlined; the label "Computer software," neither underlined nor enclosed in quotation marks; the distributor; and the year of publication. Separate items with periods, but place a comma between distributor and year of publication.

At the end of the entry add any other pertinent information— for example, the computer for which the software was designed, the number of units of memory, and the form of the program. Separate these items with commas and end the entry with a period:

> Peterson, David. *Mail Games*. Computer software. Creative Software, 1981. Atari 400/800, 32KB, disk.

When the name of the software writer is not known, begin with the title of the program:

> *Connections*. Computer software. Krell Software, 1982.

On-line information sources.
Material from an on-line (computer) information source such as DIALOG is treated like printed material, but with a reference to the source at the end of the entry. This reference should include the name of the source and identifying numbers provided by the source:

> Howard, R. K. "Chess Games and the Early Adolescent." *Elementary Education*. 27:6 (June 1983), 88-93. DIALOG file 123, item 177000 061823.

Legal references.
If you must have many references to legal documents, consult the Harvard Law Review Association's *Uniform System of Citation*. Otherwise do not use underlining or quotation marks with the titles of laws, acts, or similar documents, and use only familiar abbreviations:

> U.S. Const. Art. 1, sec. 1.
> Section 14955 of the California Government Code.

When referring to the United States Code, the title number precedes the code:

> 12 U.S.C.

Court cases are italicized:

> *Johnson v. Leatherby*

Annotated entries. Some bibliographies contain annotated entries. When you write an annotation, align its left edge to be even with the indented lines of the main bibliographic entry, and insert double the usual spacing between the main entry and the annotation:

Gowers, Ernest. *The Complete Plain Words*. Revised ed. London: Her Majesty's Stationery Office, 1973.

Although directed to English civil servants, *The Complete Plain Words* offers excellent advice to any writer.

Repeated entries. When several works by the same author are listed in sequence, you may repeat the author's name. An alternative, which will require the reader to glance back up the page, is to list the author's name at the first entry only and from then on use a line of five hyphens in place of the author's name. If the manuscript is typeset, the printer will change the five hyphens to a long dash. Alphabetical arrangement is by title, and a period follows the line of hyphens:

Catton, Bruce. *Grant Takes Command*. Boston: Little, Brown and Co., 1969.
————. *This Hallowed Ground: The Story of the Union Side of the Civil War*. Garden City, N.Y.: Doubleday & Company, Inc., 1956.

9.4 Name-and-Page-Number System

A bibliography is a good place to start, for it shows readers the source material behind the project. Nevertheless, a bibliography by itself does not enable you to make specific in-text references.

One of the easiest ways to make in-text references is to use the name-and-page-number system. Here *name* refers to the individual or organization that prepared the document listed in the bibliography. The page number is that page in the document that is the precise source of information found in the text.

A bibliography such as shown in section 9.3 is used with the name-and-page-number system. A typical in-text entry is the following one:

It is important to remember that language is not an isolated phenomenon (Hayakawa 38).

That reference pertains to page 38 of this bibliography entry:

Hayakawa, S. I. *Language in Thought and Action*. 4th ed. New York: Harcourt Brace Jovanovich, 1978.

Punctuation with in-text references.

The in-text reference is placed in parentheses, with no punctuation between name and page number. The parenthetical references come before ending or separating punctuation but after quotation marks:

It is important to remember that language is not an isolated phenomenon (Hayakawa 38).

Language is not an isolated phenomenon (Hayakawa 38), which is an important point to remember.

"Throughout this book, it is important to remember that we are not considering language as an isolated phenomenon" (Hayakawa 38).

Cross-reference: For more on the placement of in-text references, see section 9.9.

One author.   The style for a publication by one author is this:

These statistics have been documented before (Harbinson 77).

Two authors.   Two authors are joined by *and*:

(Mahoney and Harbinson 131)

Three authors. Use commas with three authors:

(Kurt, O'Neill, and Ruder 211)

More than three authors. For more than three authors, the expression "and others" or "et al." is used:

(Hasan and others 46)

Organization as author. When an organization is the author, a shortened name may be used. Thus National Bureau of Standards could become:

(Bureau of Standards 47)

Citation by title. When no author is listed, some works have to be cited by title:

(*Air Pollution Primer* 39)

More than one work in a single reference. When you cite more than one work in a single reference, use semicolons to separate them:

(Harbinson 85; Takegada 77)

Two or more works by the same author. If the bibliography shows two or more works by the same author, the in-text citation will have to show the title of the work referenced:

(Bernstein, *The Careful Writer* 47)

Two or more citations to the same author. A comma separates two or more citations to the same author:

(Hersheimer 7-10, 23-47)

Showing volume number. If it is necessary to show volume number, place the volume number
directly after the name. Follow volume number with a colon
and then the page number or numbers:

(Gershwin and Jones 1:16-21)

References not in parentheses. Paren-
theses are not necessary around parts of the citation that can
be incorporated directly into the text:

Brinkley (75-76) says just the opposite.

Brinkley says just the opposite (75-76).

9.5 Name-and-Year System

The name-and-year system is a relatively easy and econom-
ical means of citing sources in the text. Central to the system
is a bibliography or reference list. The reference list is arranged alphabetically and the items are similar to the items
shown in section 9.3, but with one major exception: The year
of publication is moved from near the end of an item to a
place just after the author's name.

Where a bibliography item looks like this:

Brinkley, Alan. *Voices of Protest: Huey Long, Father
Coughlin, and the Great Depression*. New York: Alfred
A. Knopf, 1982.

the same entry prepared for a name-and-year system would
appear with the year of publication after the author's name
and set off by periods:

Brinkley, Alan. 1982. *Voices of Protest: Huey Long, Father Coughlin, and the Great Depression*. New York:
Alfred A. Knopf.

Punctuation with in-text references.

To show the reference in text, the author's last name and the year of publication are placed in parentheses at the point desired. Within the parentheses, no punctuation separates author from year.

An author-year citation is placed before ending or separating punctuation but after quotation marks:

> The solution assumed a full fluid film with angularity and eccentricity of mating surfaces (Findley 1967).

> Shaft vibration is also a problem (Symonds 1974), which should be considered, especially in coolant pumps.

> This combination results in a large "distortion coefficient" (Yerkes 1982).

Cross-reference: For more on the placement of in-text references, see section 9.9.

One author.

The style for a publication by one author is this:

> The only major study (Brinkley 1982) says just the opposite.

or An exactly opposing point is made by the only major study of the period (Brinkley 1982).

Two authors.

For two authors, the names are joined by *and*; no separating punctuation is used:

> (Fadiman and Howard 1979)

Three authors.

For three authors, the style is as shown here:

> (Martin, Roberts, and Collins 1968)

More than three authors. For more than three authors, the expression "and others" or "et al." is used:

(Hasan and others 1983)

Authors with the same last name. In a reference to authors with the same last name, the name is repeated:

(Christensen and Christensen 1978)

Organization as author. An organization as author is shown the same as an individual author:

(National Institute of Education 1983)

Page and volume numbers. To show a page number, use a comma between it and the year:

(Christensen and Christensen 1978, 45)

The abbreviations "p." or "pp." are not necessary except to avoid confusion.

When it is necessary to show volume and page number, separate the two with a colon:

(Johnson and Johnson 1957, 3:237)

When referring to a volume alone with no page number, you will have to use "vol." so readers will know that you're not referring to a page number:

(Johnson and Johnson 1957, vol. 3)

Two or more references. Two or more references given together are separated by semicolons:

(Brinkley 1982; Martin, Roberts, and Collins, 1968; Hasan and others, 1983)

Works by the same author. When the
reference list contains several works by the same author,
show the author's name at the first entry only. From then on
use a line of five hyphens in place of the author's name.

For publications by an author in the same year, establish a
sequence by using *a*, *b*, *c*, and so on after the year:

> Charrow, R., and Charrow, V. 1978. *The Comprehension of Standard Jury Instructions: A Psycholinguistic Approach*. Arlington, Va.: Center for Applied Linguistics.
> ─────. 1979a. "Characteristics of the Language of Jury Instructions." Paper presented at the Georgetown Roundtable on Language and Linguistics. Washington, D.C.
> ─────. 1979b. "Making Legal Language Understandable: Physcholinguistic Study of Jury Instructions." *Columbia Law Review*. Vol. 79, 1306-1374.

An in-text reference to those three documents would look
like the example below. The authors' names are not repeated
for each document, and the items are separated by commas:

> (Charrow and Charrow 1978, 1979a, 1979b)

If you had to include page numbers, you would use semicolons to separate items:

> (Charrow and Charrow 1978, 31; 1979a, 14; 1979b, 7)

References not in parentheses. Parentheses are not necessary when you can incorporate all or part
of the citation in the sentence:

> Brinkley (1982) says just the opposite.

or Brinkley's 1982 work makes the opposite point.

9.6 Numbered Text References

Numbered text references are not to be confused with notes, the latter being the subject of section 9.7.

Instead, numbered text references are a variation of two other systems covered in this chapter—the name-and-page-number system (section 9.4) and the name-and-year system (section 9.5). With all three systems, a reference list or bibliography is placed at the end of the document. Other similarities and differences are shown in this table:

Numbered system	*Name systems*
Reference list is organized alphabetically or in order of first appearance of a source in text.	Reference list is organized alphabetically.
Items in the reference list are numbered.	Items in the reference list are not numbered.
Source number is given in text.	Source name is given in text.

Reference list style. With numbered text references, the reference list follows this style, which is adapted from *IEEE Communications* (July 1984):

1. DeSousa, M. R. "Electronic Information Interchange in an Office Environment." *IBM Systems Journal.* 20:1 (1981), 4-22.
2. Shick T., and Brockish, R. F. "The Document Interchange Architecture: A Member of a Family of Architectures in the SNA Environment." *IBM Systems Journal.* 21:2 (1982), 220-244.
3. Atkins, J. D. "Path Control: The Transport Network of SNA." *IEEE Transactions in Communications.* COM-28, No. 4 (1980), 527-538.
4. Gray, J. P., and McNeill, T. B. "SNA Multiple-System Networking." *IBM Systems Journal.* 18:2 (1979), 263-297.

In this reference list, the sources are not arranged alphabetically. Source 1 is the first source cited in the text, source 2 is the second source cited, source 3 is the third, and so on.

Punctuation with numbered text references.

The basic form of a numbered text reference consists of a number placed inside brackets. The combination is placed before any ending or separating punctuation but after quotation marks. Parentheses may be used in place of brackets.

The solution assumed a full fluid film with angularity and eccentricity of mating surfaces [19].

Shaft vibration is also a problem [24], which should be considered, especially in coolant pumps.

The combination results in a large "distortion coefficient" [71].

Cross-reference: For more on the placement of numbered references, see section 9.9.

One source.

When one source is cited in text, the source's number is placed in brackets and inserted into the sentence:

Credit Suisse is only to install new text systems today which conform to SNA standards and, ideally, to IBM's new architectures for text DCA [1] and DIA [2].

More than one source.

When two sources are cited, place both inside the brackets and use commas or semicolons as the marks of separation:

The following key functions were promised: alternate routing, multiple trunk circuits between network modes, . . . for example power on [3, 4].

Inclusive citations.   An inclusive list of sources is shown with a hyphen:

The use of spread-spectrum methods to combat multipath interferences is well known [3-7].

Compound references.   A compound reference allows you to refer to volume and page number without placing them in text.

In the reference list a compound reference takes this form:

Ostroff, Mark. *Composite Beam Theory*. 2 vols. Boston: Technical Press, 1979.
  9.   Vol. 1, pages 97-99.   12.   Vol. 2, pages 77-78.
10.   Vol. 1, pages 217-218.13.   Vol. 2, pages 210-219.
11.   Vol. 2, pages 18-20.   14.   Vol. 2, page 311.

In text the numbers 9 through 14 would appear in brackets.

If page numbers only were used the compound reference would read "Pages 18-20."

Subsequent citations.   If you have to refer to the same numbered reference more than once, do not construct a new item just so that the sequence is continuous throughout the text. In other words, it would be better to refer to [5] more than once in an article than to repeat the facts of publication at several points in the reference list, with each point being assigned a new number.

9.7 Notes Keyed to Superior Numbers

Notes such as those mentioned here are called *footnotes* when they are placed at the bottom of the page and *endnotes* when they are placed at the end of a chapter or book. The term used here is the more general one, *notes*.

A note is called to the reader's attention by use of a

number typed slightly above the line (a superior number or superscript).[1] Notes are numbered consecutively throughout an article or a chapter of a book.

The superior number refers to a specific page or pages in the publication listed in the notes.

Punctuation with superior numbers.

Superior numbers follow all punctuation marks except the dash:

"This is all that was offered."[1]

(For the most recent trend, see the annual supplement.)[2]

Bernstein says so[3]—as do many others.

Shaft vibration is also a problem,[4] which should be considered, especially in coolant pumps.

When more than one superior number must be used, place a comma between each number so that [1,2] will not be misread as something else.[12]

Cross-reference: For more on the placement of in-text references, see section 9.9.

Book by one author. Note style for a book by one author follows this example:

1. J. B. Bury, *The Idea of Progress: An Inquiry into Its Origin and Growth* (New York: Macmillan, 1932), 111-121.

Book by two authors. For a book by two authors, the authors named are joined by *and*:

2. Clifton Fadiman and James Howard, *Empty Pages: A Search for Writing Competency in School and Society* (Belmont, Calif.: Fearon Pitman Publishers, Inc., 1979), 17.

Book by three or more authors.
For three or more authors, commas are used to separate names:

3. Kurt Hanks, Larry Belliston, and Dave Edwards, *Design Yourself!* (Los Altos, Calif.: William Kaufmann, Inc., 1978), 17-19.

When there are more than three authors, it is permissible to shorten the reference by using "and others" or "et al."

4. Richard Bradock and others, *Research in Written Composition* (Urbana, Ill.: National Council of Teachers of English, 1963), 88-91.

Book by authors with the same last name.
When authors have the same last name, repeat the name:

5. Francis Christensen and Bonniejean Christensen, *Notes Toward a New Rhetoric: Nine Essays for Teachers*, 2d ed. (New York: Harper & Row Publishers, Inc., 1978), 22.

Book by an organization.
For a book by an organization, the note style is the same as for a note by a single author:

6. Office of Technology Assessment, *The Effects of Nuclear War* (Washington, D.C.: U.S. Government Printing Office, 1979), 9-13.

Book by an author with a pen name.
Follow the style for a book by a single author and use the pen name if that is what the book's title page shows.

Book with author's name not given.
If the author's name is known but not given on the title page, the bibliography entry shows the name in brackets. Note that the comma goes outside the brackets:

7. [Charles Harrington], *The Deacon's Surprise, and Other Follies* (London 1783), 6-8.

If the name of the author involves guesswork, a question mark is placed inside the brackets:

8. [Charles Harrington?], *The Deacon's Surprise, and Other Follies* (London 1783), 6-8.

If the author's name (or the name of the editor, compiler, or translator) is neither given nor ascertainable, begin the bibliography entry with the title of the work. Do not use "anon." or "anonymous":

9. *Environmental Quality* (Washington, D.C.: U.S. Government Printing Office, 1978), 435.

Book with editor, compiler, or translator in place of author.
A note begins with the name of the book's editor, compiler, or translator when one of these is listed on the title page and no author's name is given. A comma separates the name from "ed." ("eds."), "comp." ("comps."), or "trans":

10. Joseph Lawlor, ed., *Computers in Composition Instruction* (Los Alamitos, Calif.: SWRL Educational Research and Development, 1982), 10.
11. Allen Mandelbaum, trans., *The Aeneid of Virgil* (New York: Bantam Books, 1971), 7-8.
12. Charles R. Cooper and Lee Odell, eds., *Research on Composing: Points of Departure* (Urbana, Ill.: National Council of Teachers of English, 1978), 99-101.

Book with editor, compiler, or translator in addition to author.
Sometimes an author's name appears on the title page along with the name of an editor, compiler, or translator. In that case, the note begins with the author's name, and the editor's, compiler's,

or translator's name appears after the title. Here the abbreviations and their meanings are "ed." (edited by), "comp." (compiled by), and "trans." (translated by). Accordingly, no plural form such as "eds." is used:

13. Mark Twain, *Adventures of Huckleberry Finn*, ed. Henry Nash Smith (Boston: Houghton Mifflin Co., 1958), vii.

Book edition, series, or volume. The edition, series, or volume identification is placed after the title of a book:

14. William C. Himstreet and Wayne Murlin Baty, *Business Communications: Principles and Methods*, 7th ed. (Boston: Kent Publishing Company, 1984), 197-213.
15. H. L. Mencken, *The American Language: An Inquiry into the Development of English in the United States*, 4th ed., corrected, enlarged, and rewritten (New York: Alfred A. Knopf, 1936), viii.
16. H. L. Mencken, *The American Language: An Inquiry into the Development of English in the United States*, supplement 1 (New York: Alfred A. Knopf, 1945), ix-xi.
17. *Handbook on California's Natural Resources*, vol. 2 (Sacramento, Calif.: Resources Agency of California, 1970), 51.
18. Brian Tierney and others, eds., *The Origins of Modern Imperialism—Ideological or Economic?* Random House Historical Issues Series, No. 19 (New York: Random House, Inc., 1967), 39-43.

Book in a reprint edition. When writing a note for a reprinted edition of a book, data on the reprinting publisher is given after data on the original publisher:

19. Ambrose Bierce, *The Devil's Dictionary* (Neale Publishing Co., 1911; reprint, New York: Dover Publications, Inc., 1958), 25.

Major reference work.

A note that cites a well-known reference work need not include the publisher's name and date and place of publication. The edition, if not the first, must be specified. In addition, references to an alphabetically organized work are not to page number but to the title of the entry:

20. *Webster's New International Dictionary*, 2d ed., "quake."
21. *Who's Who in America*, 40th ed., "Flesch, Rudolf."

Biblical references.

References to the Bible should include book, chapter, and verse. A colon or a period may be used between chapter and verse. Book titles may be abbreviated:

22. Gen. 7:8-11
23. 2 Cor. 8.4

Unpublished work.

A thesis, dissertation, or book in draft is an unpublished work. Its title is placed in quotation marks, not italics, and it is identified with the word *thesis* or similar:

24. Thomas H. Willoughby, "Student Evaluation of California State Service," M.A. thesis (Sacramento, Calif.: California State University, Sacramento, 1959), 77.

Other unpublished sources include interviews, letters, memos, and telephone calls. These can be handled according to the styles shown here:

25. Johnson to Davis, letter, August 17, 1986.
26. Telephone conversation with the author, January 15, 1983.
27. Interview conducted by the author, May 17 through 20, 1979.

Articles.   When listing articles in notes, the sequence is author's name, title of the article in quotation marks, title of the periodical underlined (italics), volume number or date or both, and the specific page reference:

28.   Isaac Asimov, "In the Game of Energy and Thermodynamics You Can't Break Even," *Smithsonian* (August 1970), 9.

29.   Stanley Angrist and Loren Hepler, "Demons, Poetry, and Life: A Thermodynamic View," *Texas Quarterly,* 10 (September 1967), 27.

30.   J. T. Pindera and Y. Sze, "Creep of Some Gasket Materials," *Transactions of the Canadian Society of Mechanical Engineers,* 1:2 (June 1972), 104.

31.   "Compact-Disc Players," *Consumer Reports,* 50:6 (June 1985), 324-325.

When citing newspapers, it is sometimes necessary to give the section number or name; these go with the page number:

32.   Francis X. Clines, "The Mother Tongue Has a Movement," *New York Times* (June 3, 1984), 8E.

33.   Miles Corwin, "A City with Its Own 'Official Language,' " *San Francisco Chronicle* (May 19, 1985), *Punch,* 3.

Work cited in another work.   A note for a reference to one work but found in another work should follow this style:

34.   Jean Houston, "Prometheus Rebound: An Inquiry into Technological Growth and Psychological Change," in *Alternatives to Growth I,* Dennis Meadows, ed. (Cambridge, Mass.: Ballinger, 1977), 274.

35.   Jane R. Walpole, "Why Must the Passive Be Damned?" *College Composition and Communication,* 30:3 (October 1979), 251, in Don Bush, "The Passive Voice Should Be Avoided—Sometimes," *Technical Communication,* 28:1 (First Quarter 1981), 19.

On-line information sources. Material
from an on-line (computer) information source is treated like
printed material, but with a reference to the source at the end
of the entry. This reference should include the name of the
source and identifying numbers provided by the source:

36. R. K. Howard, "Chess Games and the Early Adolescent," *Elementary Education*, 27:6 (June 1983), 91. DIALOG file 123, item 177000 061823.

Full and shortened references. The
first time a reference is given, a full citation is used. Subsequent citations to the same source should be shortened. Usually all that is necessary is the author's last name, a short
title, and the page number. Ellipsis points are not used to
show any deleted material. Examples of full and shortened
references are:

37. John Herman Randall, *The Making of the Modern Mind* (Cambridge, Mass.: Houghton Mifflin, 1940), 33.
38. Randall, *Modern Mind*, 59.
39. Nicholaus Georgescu-Roegen, "The Steady State and Ecological Salvation," *Bio Science* (April 1977), 269.
40. Georgescu-Roegen, "Ecological Salvation," 268.

The method demonstrated in notes 37 through 40 is contrary
to the older method that relies on Latin abbreviations such as
ibid. ("the same place") or *op. cit.* ("in the work cited").

Use of the older method poses two problems. One, many
modern readers do not know Latin well enough to crack the
code at first glance. Two, when a short title is not given, as is
the case when Latin abbreviations are used, the reader may
have to glance back through several lines or even pages of
notes to find out just what work is being referred to.

Combined references. When several references are combined in one note, the individual sources are
separated by semicolons:

41.   John Herman Randall, *The Making of the Modern Mind* (Cambridge, Mass.: Houghton Mifflin, 1950), 33; Francis X. Clines, "The Mother Tongue Has a Movement," *New York Times* (June 3, 1984), 8E; and Stanley Angrist and Loren Hepler, "Demons, Poetry, and Life: A Thermodynamic View," *Texas Quarterly*, 10 (September 1967), 27.

Comments in notes.   Writers sometimes place comments in notes. This is a questionable practice, for the notes can be several hundred pages from the text to which the comment refers, and readers are usually better served if the comments are part of the text.

Nevertheless, the practice does exist. If used, the comments are written in ordinary sentence structure, and footnote style is incorporated:

42.   War Department records in the National Archives, Washington, D.C., indicate that King's real name was Anthony Cook and at the time of his death he held the rank of corporal, although almost all sources refer to him as Sergeant King. See Miller and Snell, *Why the West Was Wild*, 321.

9.8 Notes Keyed to Page Numbers

Writers of books prepared for the general public often use a form of documentation that does not intrude into the text. That is, no author-date citation or superior number or any other form is seen on text pages.

Instead, a list of references at the back of the book is keyed to a page number and a statement on that page. Styles vary from author to author. A representative example is made up of these items from John Naisbitt's *Megatrends*.

Page 241 of *Megatrends* contains these statements:

"Once upon a time . . . mustard came in two flavors— French and Gulden's," writes Marian Burros, the *New York Times* food editor . . . .

Ethnic foods now account for one-third of the 1,768 frozen foods introduced in the last five years.

The "Notes" section of *Megatrends* contains the documentation shown here. The number at the left of the entry is the page number:

241   Marian Burros on multiple-option food: "Specialty Food Explosion: Where Will It End?" the *New York Times*, October 26, 1981.
241   Ethnic frozen foods: "Ethnic Foods Accounted," *The Wall Street Journal*, December 3, 1981.

Although source page numbers are lacking, enough information is provided to enable readers to track down the source.

9.9 Placement of In-Text References

In-text references can take forms such as the author-date reference (Jones 1980), the numbered text reference [1], or the superior number.[1]

How these references are presented can affect the readability and accuracy of what you are writing.

Placement for readability. Readability simply refers to how easy it is to read a piece of writing. Generally speaking, reading ease can be improved by leaving in-text references until the end of a sentence:

Several papers deal with the mechanism of film generation in face seals [7-12].

In other words, you shouldn't break up the flow of information by inserting references in the middle of a sentence.

Placement for accuracy. When an in-text reference appears at the end of a sentence, all the reader knows is that the reference relates to something in the sen-

tence. That something could be the first word, a phrase in the middle, or a thought near or at the end.

Consequently, the accurate use of references requires that they be placed by the item to which they directly relate. This means that references will on occasion have to be placed in the middle or some other part of a sentence.

As an example of questionable placement, the reference number in this next sentence could refer to the overall statement or the different facts presented in the sentence:

> The clamped design was followed by the fully molded seal of the 1950s and the bonded seal of the 1960s [7].

Conceivably a more accurate presentation might be this one:

> The clamped design was followed by the fully molded seal of the 1950s [7] and the bonded seal of the 1960s.

And the possibility exists that the sentence should have three references:

> The clamped design [6] was followed by the fully molded seal of the 1950s [7] and the bonded seal of the 1960s [8].

That same sentence written with author-date citations would look like this:

> The clamped design (Smith 1947) was followed by the fully molded seal of the 1950s (Jones 1967) and the bonded seal of the 1960s (Johnson 1971).

Or with superior numbers:

> The clamped design[14] was followed by the fully molded seal of the 1950s[15] and the bonded seal of the 1960s.[16]

When the system of notes and superior numbers is used, as opposed to author-date or numbered references, a single superior number can be placed at the end of the sentence and all references written into one note. Thus the reader would see this sentence:

> The clamped design was followed by the fully molded seal of the 1950s and the bonded seal of the 1960s.[14]

And the lone number would direct the reader to a note that combined pertinent references:

14. For the clamped design, see J. W. Koppers, "Fluid Sealing," *Hydraulics,* 7:2 (February 1941), 77; for the fully molded seal, see R. L. Symons, "Optimum Seal Design," *Transactions of the SAE* (1963), 642-646; and for the bonded seal, see W. D. Anderson, "Bonded Seals and Their Uses," *Lubrication Engineering,* 14:1 (July 1983), 77-79.

Which way to go?

In a document on a nontechnical subject and with few references, the in-text references can probably be placed at the ends of sentences; readability is served. But in a technical document with numerous references, the in-text references are best placed directly after the item they refer to, even if that placement is in the middle of a sentence; accuracy is served.

When it comes to the placement of in-text references, you may not be able to have both accuracy and readability. In essence, the choice is yours.

Placement with quotations.

Ideally, an in-text reference follows a quotation, whether the quotation is long or short or run into the text or block indented:

> "If you scribble your thoughts any which way, your readers will surely feel that you care nothing for them."[1]

On occasion, the reference may be placed after an author's name or statement leading to the quotation:

Kurt Vonnegut's words will serve as an excellent introduction to this chapter:[1]

> Why should you examine your writing style with the idea of improving it? Do so as a mark of respect for your readers. If you scribble your thoughts any which way, your readers will surely feel that you care nothing for them.

9.10 Indentation, Alignment, and Spacing

Most documentation is typed on separate sheets that are placed at the end of the manuscript. If the work is to be published and if the documentation consists of footnotes, the printer will determine where to place the footnotes.

Exception: Footnotes for a thesis or dissertation, which are considered unpublished works, are sometimes typed at the bottom of the page of text.

Indentation, alignment, and spacing follow the guidelines given here.

Indentation and alignment. Documentation is typed using hanging indentation. That is, the first line of each entry begins at the left margin, and subsequent lines are indented according to these guidelines:

- For an unnumbered reference list, place the first letter of each line against the left margin. In the same entry, indent all lines other than the first.
- For a numbered reference list, place the numeral against the left margin. Place a period after the numeral, leave two blank spaces, and begin typing the first line. Subsequent lines in the same entry are aligned under the first letter of the first line.

When a numbered list contains more than nine items, vertical alignment will have to be made on the periods following note numbers. The largest number is placed against the left margin.

  1.   ....

 10.   ....

101.   ....

Vertical spacing.   Documentation is typed double-spaced throughout, within entries and between entries.

Exception: For a thesis or dissertation, notes are sometimes typed single-spaced at the bottom of the page of text. In this case, footnotes are separated from the text by, in this order, two blank lines and a solid, horizontal line 15 spaces long starting at the left margin:

Last line of text on the page

———————————

1.   First footnote begins here.

Horizontal spacing.   Horizontal spacing follows this style:

- After ending punctuation, leave two spaces.
- After a comma or semicolon, leave one space.
- Before and after a dash or a hyphen, leave no space.
- When a colon is used with volume and series or page number, leave no space (2:21-25).
- Before an opening (initial) parenthesis or bracket, leave one space.
- Between the opening parenthesis or bracket and the first character following, leave no space.
- Before a closing parenthesis or bracket, leave no space.
- After a closing parenthesis or bracket, (1) leave no space before any following punctuation, or (2) leave one space before the first character following.

9.11 Further Reference

Additional information on documentation can be found in the Modern Language Association's *MLA Handbook for Writers of Research Papers* and Mary-Claire van Leunen's *Handbook for Scholars*.

Chapter 10. Multiple Marks Together; Ending Punctuation

Because ending punctuation sometimes requires the use of two marks, this chapter provides instructions and examples in two areas: the use of multiple marks together and the use of punctuation suitable at the end of a sentence.

Related topics covered elsewhere in the book include:

10.1 Multiple Punctuation: General

When two different marks of punctuation could occur at the same location in a sentence, the stronger mark is used:

Who shouted, ''Run up the flag!'' (No question mark at end.)

''Run up the flag!'' was the shout. (No comma after ''flag.'')

The consecutive use of the same mark usually does not pose problems. For instance, commas to separate items in a series are standard, as in 1, 2, 3, and 4. However, the use of parentheses inside parentheses looks strange, and writers should work to avoid such combinations. And to prevent confusion, you should not use more than two dashes in a sentence.

10.2 Punctuation with Parentheses

The basic rules for punctuation with parentheses are these:

1. (When a complete sentence is enclosed in parentheses, place ending punctuation inside the parentheses, like this.)
2. When only part of a sentence is enclosed in parentheses (like this), place ending punctuation outside the parentheses (like this).

Some examples:

The first pig died. (It had refused to eat.)

or The first pig died (the one that refused to eat).

or without parentheses

The pig that refused to eat died.

Convert European date forms (28 Aug. 1983) to conventional (Aug. 28, 1983).

Can anyone forget—or forgive—*Zardoz* (1974)?

Exception: For when not to use ending punctuation, see section 10.4.

A period after an abbreviation stays with its abbreviation, in this case, inside the parentheses:

He is a Springfield (Ill.) Republican.

If required by sentence structure, other punctuation may follow a closing parenthesis:

The rich Ukraine, including Kiev (the Orthodox mother of all Russian cities), was ceded to little Poland.

or The rich Ukraine—including Kiev (the Orthodox mother of all Russian cities)—was ceded to little Poland.

Lab technicians became concerned about changes in the animals (four pigs): All of the four had become restless during the night.

They used the European date form (28 Aug. 1983); it should be converted to conventional (Aug. 28, 1983).

10.3 Punctuation with Italics

When an expression is placed in italics (underlined), the punctuation that immediately follows is treated similarly:

Why are we talking about the *cosmos?*

10.4 Ending Punctuation Not Used

A sentence within a sentence. Don't use a period at the end of a sentence within another sentence:

Her statement, ''I was late because of a flat tire,'' was not believed.

The sarcasm in his voice (you could hardly fail to notice it) did not set well with the crowd.

or The sarcasm in his voice—you could hardly fail to notice it— did not set well with the crowd.

Exception: When the sense of an interior sentence calls for a question mark or an exclamation mark, these should be retained:

She cried—had she been crying all night?—and the nurse went to her side.

I writhed on the floor in pain—damn, it hurts!—until the shot took effect.

Heading on a line by itself. No ending punctuation is used after any heading or subheading on a line by itself.

But a period follows a heading or subheading that is run into the first line of a paragraph. This type of heading is known as a *run-in sidehead*. Run-in sideheads are italicized or set in bold-faced type or bold-faced italics.

For example, see the styles of headings used in this book.

10.5 Ending Punctuation and Abbreviations

A period is used after some abbreviations: *Dr.*, *Mr.*, *Mrs.*, *Ms*.

Do not double the period when a sentence ends with an abbreviation:

He invaded Greece in 475 B.C. (No need to write "B.C..")

The plane arrives at 2 p.m.

The normal range is 200 to 800 pg/ml.

But the requirements are different when the abbreviation includes an exponent:

The volume of the room was calculated at 1,200 ft.^{3}

10.6 Ending Punctuation with Correspondence

The closing of a letter is punctuated with a comma:

Please give us a call when you have time. We'd be pleased to work with you again.
Best wishes,
[signature]

Cross-reference: To punctuate the opening of a letter, see section 1.11.

10.7 To End a Statement

A declarative sentence ends with a period:

The solution needs to be filtered.

So does an imperative sentence that is not exclamatory:

Filter the solution.

Some other examples of statements that end with periods, not exclamation marks or question marks:

Yes.

Let's go now.

That is the normal range for levels of vitamin B_{12}.

That is the normal range for levels of vitamin B_{12}.[4]

Tour the serene Yolo farmlands and the rolling Capay hills where camels and llamas abide.

10.8 To End a Question

Questions come in two types—direct and indirect.

To end a direct question.   Use a question mark to end a direct question:

Who's taking the money?

Where do I pay?

Who's taking the money? And where do I pay?

or   Who's taking the money, and where do I pay?

You're not upset, are you?

You're not upset?

How did this happen? was the question on everyone's lips.

A direct question can also be used to parenthetically question the accuracy of a statement:

He was chief of staff for many years (21?).

But that sentence would read better if recast without the question mark:

He was chief of staff for approximately 21 years.

To end an indirect question.   An indirect question ends with a period:

He was honest enough to ask where he should pay.

She asked herself why.

How this could happen was the question on everyone's lips.

10.9 To End an Exclamation

An exclamation, outcry, or emphatic comment ends with an exclamation mark. Writers should take pains to use this mark sparingly:

Help!

I can't believe I finished the whole thing!

Boy, am I glad that's over!

Whew!

Bibliography

Primary Sources

American Institute of Physics. *Style Manual for Guidance in the Preparation of Papers for Journals Published by the American Institute of Physics*. 3d ed. New York: American Institute of Physics, 1978.

American Medical Association. *Stylebook/Editorial Manual*. Littleton, Massachusetts: Publishing Sciences Group, 1976.

American Psychological Association. *Publication Manual of the American Psychological Association*. 3d ed. Washington D.C.: American Psychological Association, 1983.

Associated Press. *The Associated Press Stylebook and Libel Manual*. Reading, Massachusetts: Addison-Wesley, 1982.

Council of Biology Editors. *CBE Style Manual: A Guide for Authors, Editors, and Publishers in the Biological Sciences*. 5th ed., revised and expanded. Bethesda, Maryland: Council of Biology Editors, 1983.

Gibaldi, Joseph, and Achtest, Walter S. *MLA Handbook for Writers of Research Papers*. 2d ed. New York: The Modern Language Association of America, 1984.

Longyear, Marie, ed. *The McGraw-Hill Style Manual: A Concise Guide for Writers and Editors*. New York: McGraw-Hill Book Company, 1983.

Skillin, Marjorie, and others. *Words into Type*. 3d ed., completely revised. Englewood Cliffs, New Jersey: Prentice-Hall, 1974.

United States Government Printing Office. *Style Manual*. Washington, D.C.: U.S. Government Printing Office, 1984.

The University of Chicago Press. *The Chicago Manual of Style*. 13th ed., revised and expanded. Chicago: The University of Chicago Press, 1982.

van Leunen, Mary-Claire. *A Handbook for Scholars*. New York: Alfred A. Knopf, 1978.

Additional Sources

Brittain, Robert. *A Pocket Guide to Correct Punctuation*. Woodbury, New York: Barron's Educational Series, 1982.

Ehrlich, Eugene. *Schaum's Outline of Theory and Problems of Punctuation, Capitalization, and Spelling*. New York: McGraw-Hill Book Company, 1977.

Gordon, Karen E. *The Well-Tempered Sentence: A Punctuation Handbook for the Innocent, the Eager, and the Doomed*. New York: Ticknor and Fields, 1983.

Harvard Law Review Association. *A Uniform System of Citation*. 13th ed. Cambridge, Massachusetts: Harvard Law Review Association, 1981.

"Judicial Decision on a Question Mark," *American Speech*, 16:4 (December 1941), 318-319.

Limaye, Mohan R. "Approaching Punctuation as a System." *ABCA Bulletin* (March 1983), 28-33.

Mellinkoff, David. *The Language of the Law*. Boston: Little, Brown and Company, 1963.

Michaelson, H. B. "How to Cite References Properly in Text." *Technical Communication* (3d quarter 1981), 20-21.

Murdock, Lindsay R. "Use of Hyphens in Unit Modifiers." *Technical Communication* (2d quarter 1982), 6-7.

Partridge, Eric. *You Have a Point There: A Guide to Punctuation and Its Allies*. London: Hamish Hamilton, 1953.

Rook, Fern. "Slaying the English Jargon: About the Hyphen." *Technical Communication* (1st quarter 1981), 27.

———. "Slaying the English Jargon: Commonplace Commas." *Technical Communication* (2d quarter 1984), 29.

———. "Slaying the English Jargon: Hyphens." *Technical Communication* (1st quarter 1985), 42.

———. "Slaying the English Jargon: Possessives." *Technical Communication* (3d quarter 1979), 29.

———. "Slaying the English Jargon: What's the Rule on the Virgule?" *Technical Communication* (2d quarter 1985), 49.

Sanderson, Dave. "Conversations with Yourself." *Writer's Digest* (September 1973), 25.

Shaw, Harry. *Punctuate It Right!* New York: Barnes & Noble, Inc., 1963.

Simon, John. "The Language: A Pointed Discussion of Punctuation." *Esquire*. 89:2 (February 1978), 16, 21.

Simpson, Percy. *Shakespearean Punctuation*. Oxford, England: Clarendon Press, 1911.

Stein, Richard. "Slaying the English Jargon: Apropos of Apostrophes." *Technical Communication* (2d quarter 1981), 29.

Treip, Mindele. *Milton's Punctuation and Changing English Usage, 1582-1676*. London: Methuen & Co., Ltd., 1970.

Index